ONLINE ACTIVISM
SOCIAL CHANGE THROUGH SOCIAL MEDIA

By Amanda Vink

Published in 2019 by
Lucent Press, an Imprint of Greenhaven Publishing, LLC
353 3rd Avenue
Suite 255
New York, NY 10010

Designer: Seth Hughes
Editor: Jennifer Lombardo

Library of Congress Cataloging-in-Publication Data

Names: Vink, Amanda, author.
Title: Online activism : social change through social media / Amanda Vink.
Description: New York : Lucent Press, [2019] | Series: Hot topics | Includes
    bibliographical references and index.
Identifiers: LCCN 2018004087| ISBN 9781534563568 (library bound book) | ISBN
    9781534563582 (pbk. book) ISBN 9781534563575 (ebook)
Subjects: LCSH: Internet–Political aspects–Juvenile literature. | Social
    media–Political aspects–Juvenile literature. | Political
    participation–Juvenile literature. | Youth–Political activity–Juvenile
    literature.
Classification: LCC HM851 .V56 2019 | DDC 302.23/1–dc23
LC record available at https://lccn.loc.gov/2018004087

Printed in the United States of America

CPSIA compliance information: Batch #BS18KL: For further information contact Greenhaven Publishing LLC, New York,
New York at 1-844-317-7404.

Please visit our website, www.greenhavenpublishing.com. For a free color catalog of all our high-quality books, call toll free 1-844-317-7404 or fax 1-844-317-7405.

CONTENTS

Adolescence is a time when many people begin to take notice of the world around them. News channels, blogs, and talk radio shows are constantly promoting one view or another; very few are unbiased. Young people also hear conflicting information from parents, friends, teachers, and acquaintances. Often, they will hear only one side of an issue or be given flawed information. People who are trying to support a particular viewpoint may cite inaccurate facts and statistics on their blogs, and news programs present many conflicting views of important issues in our society. In a world where it seems everyone has a platform to share their thoughts, it can be difficult to find unbiased, accurate information about important issues.

It is not only facts that are important. In blog posts, in comments on online videos, and on talk shows, people will share opinions that are not necessarily true or false, but can still have a strong impact. For example, many young people struggle with their body image. Seeing or hearing negative comments about particular body types online can have a huge effect on the way someone views himself or herself and may lead to depression and anxiety. Although it is important not to keep information hidden from young people under the guise of protecting them, it is equally important to offer encouragement on issues that affect their mental health.

The titles in the Hot Topics series provide readers with different viewpoints on important issues in today's society. Many of these issues, such as teen pregnancy and Internet safety, are of immediate concern to young people. This series aims to give readers factual context on these crucial topics in a way that lets them form their own opinions. The facts presented throughout also serve to empower readers to help themselves or support people they know who are struggling with many of the challenges adolescents face today. Although negative viewpoints are not ignored or downplayed, this series allows young people to see that the challenges they face are not insurmountable. Eating disorders can be overcome, the Internet can be navigated safely, and pregnant teens do not have to feel hopeless.

Quotes encompassing all viewpoints are presented and cited so readers can trace them back to their original source, verifying for themselves whether the information comes from a reputable place. Additional books and websites are listed, giving readers a starting point from which to continue their own research. Chapter questions encourage discussion, allowing young people to hear and understand their classmates' points of view as they further solidify their own. Full-color photographs and enlightening charts provide a deeper understanding of the topics at hand. All of these features augment the informative text, helping young people understand the world they live in and formulate their own opinions concerning the best way they can improve it.

The Arab Spring

On January 25, 2011, thousands of protesters crowded the streets of Cairo and several other Egyptian cities to demand freedom from a corrupt political regime. This became known as the Egyptian Revolution. Three months earlier, the National Democratic Party led by President Hosni Mubārak had celebrated a landslide victory in an election that was not fair. On the day of the protests, the downtown plaza of Cairo, Tahrir Square, was flooded with people standing shoulder to shoulder and holding signs of discontent. Some people argue it was social media that helped the crowd organize and get there.

A significant portion of the protesters—28.3 percent—who came out to Tahrir Square heard about the demonstrations on Facebook. The spread of information by Facebook was second only to word-of-mouth. According to the website Journalist's Resource, 52 percent of the protesters had a Facebook profile. The majority of them used their social media influence to spread the word about the demonstrations, and many posted videos as protesters began to clash with police forces. Twitter was also used during these protests. One activist tweeted 60,000 words over the course of the revolution.

Social media was a major influencer in the Egyptian Revolution and the Arab Spring movement, which was the name given to the multiple protests and revolutions that occurred in the Middle East and North Africa around the same time. Mubārak had been the leader of Egypt since 1981, when he rose to power after the assassination of President Anwar el-Sādāt. Upon taking power, he issued a state of emergency that was never lifted. This state of emergency expanded police power and made the censorship of media standard. Opposition to the

Egyptian protestors are shown here on their way to Tahrir Square in 2011.

government was quickly weeded out, and tensions steadily rose between the citizens and the police state.

A year before the protests, in June 2010, 28-year-old Khaled Said was beaten to death by the police. By his relatives' accounts, his bluetooth picked up a video of police sharing seized narcotics and cash from the internet cafe below his residence. Said shared the video with his friends, and it was then shared with more people. It was two of the implicated policemen who seized him outside his residence, brought him into the internet cafe, and beat him to death. The initial report said the cause of death was severe cardiovascular asphyxiation, which was supposedly caused by a high level of drugs in his system. Said's relatives were suspicious, and they received a photo of Said's body by bribing a guard at the morgue. That photo was posted online, and it quickly spread. It showed Said's face, which had been broken and distorted by the deadly blows.

Following this event, a Facebook page was created called "We Are All Khaled Said." The Facebook page was run by an individual who went by the pseudonym El Shaheed, which means "the martyr" in Arabic. It was not the only Facebook page created—14,000 Facebook pages and 32,000 Facebook groups were created in Egypt in the 2 weeks leading up to the protests and in the initial days of the protests in Tahrir Square.

"We Are All Khaled Said" started to collect followers. By educating people and encouraging them to speak about their concerns about police brutality, the abuse of government power, and the economic struggles of many individuals, the page created a space for solidarity. The steadily growing number of followers began to organize, and they made it known they were ready for a change. After Tunisia's leader, President Zine el-Abidine Ben Ali, stepped down, Egyptians were spurred into action. If the people of another country could demand freedom, why could the Egyptians not do the same?

The protesters came to Tahrir Square, and online, they used the hashtag #Jan25. "Tahrir was a space of unity, pride, resistance, celebration, laughter, sharing, and most importantly ownership," wrote Alex Nunns and Nadia Idle in the book *Tweets from Tahrir: Egypt's Revolution as it Unfolded, in the Words of the People Who Made It.* "This was the People's space; our rules and our demands. We would not leave until justice was born."[1]

The response of the government was to increase military involvement, and things turned violent quickly. At Tahrir Square, police used tear gas and water cannons. Rocks and sticks were thrown. After nightfall, the police added rubber bullets to their weapons.

A sign at a protest depicts Khaled Said, whose death inspired the Facebook page that helped start the Egyptian revolution.

On Wednesday, January 26, 2011, after the massive turn-out at Tahrir Square, authorities cut some communications websites through mobile devices. During this five-day internet blackout, activists did anything they could to get online. Some called friends in other countries to ask them to post tweets or made offers to news organizations that they would give them an interview if they could have access to the organization's satellite internet connections.

On the evening of January 26, Google's head of marketing in the Middle East, Wael Ghonim, gave an interview on a popular talk show in Egypt to criticize internet censorship. The next night, he disappeared. It came out during the next week that Ghonim had been the creator of the Facebook page "We Are All Khaled Said." When he was released from detention after nearly two weeks, Ghonim discovered that he had become one of the faces of the revolution. While Ghonim has used this position to talk about the role of social media in activism—for example, his 2015 TED Talk called "Let's Design Social Media That Drives Real Change"—he continues to be a somewhat reluctant figurehead.

Just after midnight on January 28, the Egyptian government ordered cell phone operators and internet service providers (ISPs) to shut down completely. The only ISP allowed to run would connect the Egyptian stock exchange with the rest of the world. This massive shutdown shows how afraid the Egyptian government had become of its citizens speaking to each other and organizing together, particularly through the use of the internet. Nunns and Idle wrote,

> Terrified of the new tools of Twitter and Facebook, and the uncensored visual media of yFrog, Flickr and Youtube, the regime chose to pay the price of millions of lost dollars to the economy in order to deprive protesters of a key weapon—the means of communication.[2]

In fact, people around the world were riveted by what they saw online about what was happening in Egypt. People all over the world felt an intense connection to what was happening because they watched it in real time.

After 18 days of protests, Mubārak stepped down on February 11, 2011.

Wael Ghonim (center) became an icon when it came to light that he was the creator of "We Are All Khaled Said." He remains outspoken about the pros and cons of social media activism.

Social Media's Role in Egypt's Revolution

In one of his TED Talks, Ghonim argued that the internet and social media "played a great role in helping these people to speak up their minds, to collaborate together … to start thinking together."[3] The numbers support this theory.

A study done by the University of Washington measured political social media use before and during the revolution. The total rate of tweets about political change rose dramatically, from 2,300 a day to 230,000 a day. The top 23 videos featuring protest and political commentary received nearly 5.5 million views.

The Arab Spring was an example of people taking back their power of communication. According to Philip Howard, the study's project leader and an associate professor of communication at the University of Washington, social media was a tool that "altered the capacity of citizens to affect domestic politics."[4]

There are people who are skeptical about social media's role in the Arab Spring. It is important to note that many Egyptians who were involved in the revolution did not have access to internet or mobile devices either before, during, or after the protests.

Documentary filmmaker Parvez Sharma argued,

> The majority of the protesters in Cairo, in Suez, in Alexandria, in Luxor, in Mahla, in Manoura, and all over this ancient land that is the very heart of what it means to be Arab, are not "twittering" or "Facebooking" or "emailing" or even watching the landmark live coverage that Al-Jazeera is providing. They are out on the streets—and yes, without phone access—risking their lives and giving vent to three decades, and perhaps more, of anger.[5]

Other critics argue that revolutions existed long before Facebook, and these individuals believe a revolution would have been pending with or without the use of social media. "People with a grievance will always find ways to communicate with each other,"[6] argued author Malcolm Gladwell after citing both the fall of East Germany during the Cold War in the 1980s and the French Revolution in the late 1700s, both of which happened before most people had access to the internet.

Going even further, some critics believe that use of social media in many cases can be harmful to revolutionary citizens. Journalist and editor Nicholas Thompson argued that citizens are not the only ones using the internet to achieve results. Governments often control the use of media. In Tunisia, for example, the government hacked the accounts of nearly every Facebook user in the country. If the leadership—Ben Ali and his party—had not fallen so quickly, the social media information gained would have been useful to the government the people were trying to overthrow.

In addition, many online protests do not have a recognizable leader. Once the government is toppled, there is a vacuum of power that becomes up for grabs. Who, then, is there to take control of the situation? Les Gelb at the *Daily Beast* noted how "in rotten regimes that fall to street mobs, the historical pattern has been moderates followed by new dictators."[7]

While the debate over the effectiveness of online activism continues, there is no denying social media played a major role in the way the story of the Arab Spring was recorded and told. As Tim Eaton of BBC Media Action explained, "Through the use of technology, and social media in particular, these events were brought into the living rooms of people across the world, enabling them to witness events in unprecedented detail and with unprecedented speed."[8]

Shown here is the fall of the Berlin Wall in 1989. The wall separated East and West Germany during the Cold War, and the demonstrations surrounding its removal were organized before the internet became widespread.

Nunns and Idle have a similar stance, arguing, "The internet provided a tool that helped shape the form of the uprising, and it gave us some of the most riveting real-time coverage ever recorded."[9] It also inspired the rest of the world to utilize social media activism.

The History of Online Activism

Social activism has been around since the beginning of organized leadership. Some scholars see a fourth-century poem by the Chinese philosopher Tao Te Ching as an activist work to speak out against greed of the wealthy elite. Some people believe that many religions teach practices of activism. There are many examples of activism throughout history, and many successful ones involved great communication skills: Writing a problem down often led to the spread of an idea and the growth of an activist movement.

The Catholic Church split during the 16th century, when the 33-year-old Augustinian friar Martin Luther wrote his *Ninety-Five Theses*—a list of issues he had with the Church—and presented it to the Church in 1517. Stories differ on whether he actually nailed the list to the church door in Saxony, Germany, or whether he sent the list to the local archbishop, but either way, he made his grievances known by writing them down for others to see. The act of declaring his criticism publicly fractured the Church, an event called the Protestant Reformation. Those who supported the Pope in Rome, Italy, were called the Roman Catholics and members of the new sect, which followed Luther's suggestions, were called the Lutherans.

Luther's activism sparked conflict in Europe: Wars broke out as rulers attempted to distance themselves from the Pope's authority in Rome. Between 1518 and 1525, Luther used the printing press to publish his ideas, which included purifying the Church—specifically by ending the practice of indulgences, in which the Pope forgave sinners in exchange for money—and making the Bible the sole point of authority when it came to questions of faith.

Martin Luther used the written word to spread controversial ideas about the Catholic religion. His writings helped bring about the Protestant Reformation.

Just as printed documents were important to Luther, printed documents propelled action during more recent historical movements. Pamphlets were an important medium in the history of the United States. In 1776, a pamphlet called "Common Sense," which argued for American independence from Britain, was published by Thomas Paine. At the time of Paine's publication, many colonists considered themselves British citizens. To declare otherwise was dangerous, yet his pamphlet sold roughly 500,000 copies and had a great impact on the colonists' way of thinking. In addition to "Common Sense," Paine also wrote "The Rights of Man," which supported the French Revolution, in 1791.

During the end of the 19th century and well into the 20th century, women fought for the right to vote in Britain and in the United States. The word "suffrage" means the right to vote in elections. When the public started to call the Women's Social and Political Union (WSPU) members "suffragettes," they named their journal *The Suffragette* in honor of the term. The newspaper was a primary tool in the effort to gain the right to vote in Britain, and it featured detailed articles and opinion pieces, visual propaganda, and organized event information.

The newspaper widely publicized the dramatic actions that were taken to gain attention and financial support for the suffragettes. Members of the WSPU held huge marches and demonstrations. More than 1,000 suffragettes were imprisoned between 1908 and 1914, and many used the imprisonment as a way to make a statement through hunger strikes, or the refusal to eat. All of these events were recorded in detail, and the movement spread.

Two suffragettes in New York are shown here posting bulletins as a way to spread the message that women should have the right to vote.

CREATING ANGER AGAINST ENGLAND

"Europe, and not England, is the parent country of America. This new world hath been the asylum for the persecuted lovers of civil and religious liberty from every part of Europe. Hither they have fled, not from the tender embraces of the mother, but from the cruelty of the monster; and it is so far true of England, that the same tyranny which drove the first emigrants from home, pursues their descendants still."

—Thomas Paine, activist

Quoted in "1776: Thomas Paine Publishes Common Sense," History.com, accessed on November 27, 2017. www.history.com/this-day-in-history/thomas-paine-publishes-common-sense.

Spreading a Message

An effective activist movement must get the word out to build a supportive following. In the above cases, printing and distribution were ways to mobilize a large number of people. The internet today is what the printing press was to the people of those earlier centuries—it is a new technology used to spread information to a vast audience.

The difference in the internet age is speed. Communication before computers and modern technology took much longer. In 1860, on the Pony Express—an organization in which people delivered mail by riding horses along the 2,000-mile (3218.7 km) route between St. Joseph, Missouri, and Sacramento, California—it took 10 days to deliver a letter. It was also expensive, costing $5 (equivalent to roughly $141 in 2018) for every 0.5 ounce (14 g) of mail delivered. Today, a post online can be published instantly, and in most cases—as long as the website does not require a paid subscription—it is free.

Other ways activists effectively communicate their goals are letter writing to newspapers and politicians, rallies, boycotts, and sit-ins. The more extreme actions are most effective when publicized by newspapers or online.

The Pony Express delivered mail through the American West. The communication method was not ideal for average people, as it was costly.

A Brief History of the Internet

After the Soviet Union launched Sputnik, the world's first man-made satellite, in 1957, Americans were convinced that advances in technology would decide the fate of the Cold War. Scientists and military leaders worried what would happen in the case of an attack on the telephone wire system, which made long-distance communication possible. In 1962, a scientist named J. C. R. Licklider came up with an idea that might solve the problem: a network of computers that could communicate with each other.

In 1969, the first message was sent between two computers. The message was broken down and then reassembled once it reached its destination. The message, the single word LOGIN, crashed the network. The computer on the receiving end only received the L and the O. Despite crashing the network, it was an incredible breakthrough, which was only the first of many to come.

By the 1980s, computer scientist Vinton Cerf figured out a way for computers to recognize each other in a virtual space. Then, in 1991, a British computer programmer named Tim

Berners-Lee introduced the World Wide Web, a "web" with information that anyone could retrieve. In 1992, the U.S. Congress opened up this web for commercial purposes. After Congress granted commercial organizations the right to use the internet for business, companies began to create their own websites.

Cables, such as those shown here, help speed up the spread of information over the internet. Newer technologies such as cell phones have allowed users to connect to the internet without wires.

The internet then became extremely important to the way modern society functions. Much of society's everyday business is conducted online. Businesses make payments and track shipments online, as well many other functions. Individuals make and receive payments online, and many people rely on the internet to keep up to date with the happenings of the world.

Baby

The first modern and recognizable computer was built in the late 1940s. The Small Scale Experimental Machine, nicknamed Baby, was very different from the modern computer. Baby was made of metal post office racks, garden fence posts, and parts left over from World War II in Europe. There was no screen. Baby had less computing power than a modern-day calculator; however, it was a breakthrough that led to all the technology available today. As of 2018, a replica of the machine, which was dismantled, is on display at the Museum of Science and Industry in Manchester, United Kingdom (UK).

This photograph shows Professor Tom Kilburn (left) and Professor Freddy Williams (right) in front of Baby, their creation.

Blogs

In 1994, Justin Hall created the first personal blog at links.net while he was a student at Swarthmore College in Pennsylvania. He did not call it a blog, though; the term "weblog" was not coined until 1997. Instead he referred to it as his personal homepage, and on it he wrote about his life—his father's alcoholism and suicide, relationships, and his coming of age stories. He has also written about how the internet made it easy for him to get published. He wrote, "I could put my writings and words up electronically, make them look pretty, and engage the web with links. And I didn't have to pay anyone to do any of it!"[10] As search engines became more popular, the blog started to affect Hall's personal relationships. He shut it down briefly to pursue a relationship with a woman who was not interested in internet fame. After the relationship was over, he reinstated the blog, which is still active as of 2018. It is the longest running blog on the internet.

In 1999, there were 23 blogs on the internet. During the 2000s, that number expanded to more than 50 million. This was the result of blog-hosting websites, which made it a lot easier for people without coding experience to create their own homepages. One such website, which is still active today, is WordPress.

It is not only individuals who publish blogs. Now, most national newspapers have blogs, which they use to share updates on news events quickly. Many businesses also have blogs as a way of attracting customers. Many blogs even have sponsors, and the blogs offer deals and link to companies to make it easy for their followers to buy products.

Search engines such as Google and Bing use algorithms—a set of rules for computers to follow, such as picking out certain keywords—to rank websites. Websites that have a higher search engine optimization (SEO) appear in the top results, and they appear first when a person searches for a particular topic. People who are trying to get more people to see their posts might consider using words that are trending.

It is important to know how the internet works, especially for an activist. First, an activist can use some of the same strategies that work to spread a message. Second, an activist should have knowledge of how the internet works so they do not get scammed or taken advantage of while attempting to promote a cause.

What Is Online Activism?

Communication through the internet can be extremely effective, although it is important to note that conversations online are difficult to control. Once something is online—especially if it goes viral—it tends to have a life of its own.

TIME magazine reported in 2015 that about 3 billion people use the internet worldwide, and of those, 2 billion are individuals from developing countries. The average American spends 10 hours per day consuming information from a screen, whether it is a desktop computer, tablet, or mobile device.

MANY TOOLS

"We have more tools than ever to make our voices heard: not only the familiar methods of attending public forums, writing to our newspapers, and calling our radio stations, but a whole array of new means powered by the Internet. We have online forums on which we can debate, blogs on which we can publish, wikis on which we can collaborate, video blogs and podcasts through which we can broadcast images and sound. Indeed, new tools roll out every day, most of them cheap, if not free. Never before have average people had greater ability to make themselves heard."

–Jon Lebowsky, author and activist

Jon Lebowsky, "Amplifying Your Voice," in *Worldchanging: A User's Guide for the 21st Century*. Alex Steffen, ed. New York, NY: Abrams, 2011. p. 392.

Online activism, also called internet activism, is the use of electronic platforms to create social or political change. The number one goal of any of these individuals or movements is to make an opinion known to a wide audience and then to convince others to support this idea. These movements can be carefully planned by activist organizations or they can be spontaneous—the result of an image or video that took off online. These campaigns can look very different from one another, and they can be used to great effect by people who have very different political viewpoints and different stances on issues.

The world is more connected than ever in the 21st century. With so many individuals using the internet as a means of communication, it is no surprise that activism has its own channels on digital mediums. One of the most important changes seen in the digital age is real-time updates and conversations. Social networking websites such as Facebook, Twitter, and Snapchat as well as other channels of communication, such as blogs, make it even easier to talk about issues and events as they are happening.

Life in a Day

In 2009, filmmakers Kevin MacDonald and Loressa Clisby, along with producer Ridley Scott, asked the world to post video footage of one day in their lives: July 24, 2010. They received 80,000 YouTube submissions, from which they curated content from people in 197 countries. *Life in a Day* is a time capsule and also an art project of the digital age. A project such as this, which relies on global crowdsourcing, would not have been possible without the internet. According to MacDonald, "The idea that you can ask thousands, tens of thousands, maybe hundreds of thousands of people all to contribute to a project and all to communicate about it and learn about it at the same time belongs essentially to this age that we live in."[1]

1. Quoted in Melissa Langdon, *The Work of Art in a Digital Age: Art, Technology and Globalisation.* New York, NY: Springer, 2014, p. 132.

Networking Websites

The first social networking website was called Six Degrees. It was built in 1996 and launched in 1997, and it was based on the idea that everyone is connected through six degrees of separation; for instance, a person knows a friend who knows a friend and so on, and that can connect a person with everyone in the world.

The main function of social networking websites is to connect people online. As such, they have become an important tool activists use to connect people to causes and organizations. They are also the platforms used most often when people share real-time videos and news coverage.

Facebook, the largest social media website, allows online activists to communicate with one another, find like-minded individuals, and organize campaigns.

The largest social networking website as of 2018, Facebook, has more than 2 billion active members. That number is growing consistently at around 17 percent per year. Experts estimate that one in every five minutes on the internet is spent on Facebook.

The Facebook—the original name of the website—was created in February 2004 by Mark Zuckerberg while he was studying at Harvard University. The website grew rapidly. In just one month, more than half of the undergraduate population at the university had a profile. It was soon expanded to other Boston, Massachusetts, universities and then all United States universities. In August 2005, the website name Facebook.com was purchased, and by September of that year, high school students started to sign up. After September 2006, the website was opened to anyone with a registered email address. Since then, it has grown exponentially.

By 2018, Facebook had an average of 1.4 billion people logging on daily to check their newsfeeds, groups, and its messaging app. Five profiles are created every second. The average time spent per Facebook visit is 20 minutes.

Campaigns Online

With so many people spending so much time online, it is no surprise that many traditional activist organizations have made the internet part of their overall strategy. Greenpeace, for example, is an environmental nonprofit organization that started in 1971, when a small team set sail in an old fishing boat to bear witness to the underwater nuclear testing by the United States near Amchitka, a tiny island off the west coast of Alaska. While the small team never made it—they were stopped before reaching their destination—the public heard about their efforts, and a year later, the island was declared a bird sanctuary.

An Online Campaign Against Being Online

The number of campaigns on the internet is extremely large, and causes are many and varied. Ironically, there is even a campaign on the internet to promote spending less time on screens. Photographer Eric Pickersgill created a series of photographs in which he took away his subjects' phones while they continued to hold their poses. The photographs are eerie, and the people in them are presented in a way that suggests they are not engaging with one another in person. The argument could be made that the people in the photos could be holding anything with the same effect, such as a book. However, it is difficult to argue that mobile devices such as phones and tablets have not had an impact on the way humans interact, and this campaign certainly brings awareness to that idea.

That small group of activists has grown into one of the best-known activist organizations. Some of the subgroups of Greenpeace have really taken to social media, such as Greenpeace Brazil. Greenpeace Brazil grew rapidly in 2012 and attracted 548,000 Twitter followers and 240,000 Facebook followers. This growth occurred due to the intense efforts of its small social media team. In 2013, Greenpeace Brazil adopted measures to curate, listen to, and act on what their supporters were saying. The result was that Greenpeace Brazil created a space for open dialogue, which attracted more supporters and more fund-raising.

Petitions

Petitions and crowdsourcing websites are another way activists spread the word about a cause. Petitions have long held a place in the activist's strategy book. By collecting a large number of signatures, activists can show policy makers there is strong support for a particular issue.

From 1787 to 1788, more than 100 petitions were presented to the British House of Commons in an attempt to ban the slave trade. In 1792, that number rose to 519 petitions. Every English county was represented in those petitions, which showed the huge public support for abolitionists. The strategy was effective: In 1792, the House of Commons voted 230 to 85 that the slave trade should be gradually abolished. Unfortunately, the political reactions to the French Revolution forced the matter to be dropped until 1806, when the Foreign Slave Trade Bill was passed. A year later, another law called the Abolition of the Slave Trade Act officially made the British Atlantic slave trade illegal.

In September 2011, the White House created a legitimate website to collect petitions. We the People is a platform where anyone can create a petition online. If the petition gathers 100,000 signatures in 30 days, the petition will be sent to the proper policy experts and an official response will be issued.

The government website states,

> Petitioning has the potential to enact real change, but it's also your fundamental right as an American citizen, and an opportunity to

connect with a community of like-minded people who are invested in making a change. Ideally, running a petition on We the People is just the start of something bigger—a long-term, robust form of civic engagement.[11]

However, there are a number of problems with online petitions. The opportunity for follow-up to issues is low, especially if online petitioning is the only strategy being used by activists. Petitioning is most effective when used at the same time as other activist measures. According to the Pew Research Center, "the White House's refusal to comment on specific cases was common."[12] Fifteen percent of all responses were similar, pointing to the website's terms of participation page. In many cases, it also took the White House significant time to respond to petitions, and in December 2017, the government took down the website altogether after ignoring it for a year. The website was relaunched in early 2018, but 17 petitions that had met the goal of 100,000 signatures within 30 days were not addressed by the White House before the website was temporarily taken down.

Shown here is the original 2,000-signature petition that supported the 1806 Foreign Slave Trade Bill, which paved the way for the Abolition of the Slave Trade Act.

In addition, there are many petitioners who do not take the online petition website seriously. For example, in 2013, a petition on We the People asked the Obama administration to build a Death Star, the space station with the ability to destroy planets from the *Star Wars* movies. The official response was that the cost was too high and that the administration did "not support blowing up planets."[13] While amusing, it took time away from the White House responding to other issues. However, it is important to point out that science and technology adviser Paul Shawcross took the response as an opportunity to teach interested parties about the projects started in the space program, such as the International Space Station that was finished in 2011.

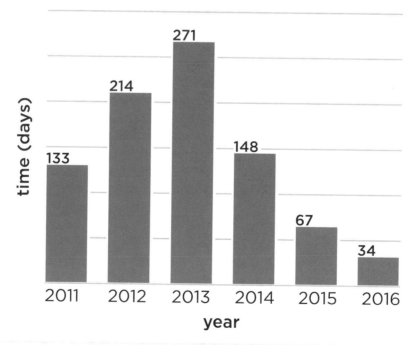

Average Wait Time for White House Response

This information from the Pew Research Center shows the average wait time for a White House response to a We the People petition.

For all its faults, We the People has done the work of allowing the U.S. government to clarify its stance on a number of issues, including responding to a petition protesting a cybersecurity bill called the Cyber Intelligence Sharing and Protection Act (CISPA)—passed by the House of Representatives in April 2013—that encouraged businesses and government agencies to share more information. As reporter Adi Robertson noted, "Questions that *were* silly still served a symbolic purpose. If enough people supported you, you could get the White House to explain its position on any issue, no matter how bizarre."[14]

The first example of a We the People petition resulting in effective action was when the White House responded to a petition to protect cell phone consumers. The petition asked the White House to make it legal for them to unlock their phones so they would work on other networks and they would not have to buy a new phone. Before 2014, when the bill was signed into law, it was illegal for people to unlock their phone; every time they switched networks, they needed to buy a new phone, which often kept people from finding the best deal on a cell phone plan due to the high cost of buying a new phone.

Is Online Activism Effective?

The effectiveness of online activism is one aspect that has been hotly debated. Critics say the internet makes it too easy to share an opinion without actually doing the work that creates change. Others argue that a single voice that shares an alternative point of view in the form of a blog post, link, or tweet could be the ripple that eventually creates a tidal wave. Political campaigns and activist movements have all been affected by the power of online communication, so much so that organizations that want to keep up with the conversations and concerns of people have found it necessary to start paying attention.

How Online Activism Works

The Arab Spring was not the first time activists used the internet to create change, but there is no denying that social media played an important role in communication during the uprisings. It also catapulted the visibility of the revolution. People all across the world were learning about this historic moment as it was happening in real time, and many activist groups later used the lessons about the power of social media they had learned during that movement. One of the key aspects of online activism is its ability to connect an incredibly large volume of people to a cause at the speed of a router.

The Sunflower Movement

When the Cross-Strait Service Trade Agreement (CSSTA), which would allow for the creation of investment opportunities across Taiwan and China, was signed into legislation in Taiwan's parliament in March 2014, a group of volunteers broke into the Executive Yuan building, the location that houses Taiwan's executive branch, as well as the Legislative Yuan building. They occupied the area for 24 days, and the demonstration brought 500,000 Taiwanese citizens out into the streets.

The use of technology was crucial during this demonstration. Volunteers set up live streaming in the parliament building. The group g0v.tw launched a website and took over the live streaming formally. The mission was to give citizens the most transparent information so they could make their own decisions about the way the country was run. Using Hackpad, which is software for the collective editing of documents, more than 1,500 volunteers worked together to share as much information as possible. The group was also able to crowd-fund more than $6 million in New Taiwan dollars ($210,000 in American currency). With that money, the Sunflower Movement continued to prioritize awareness to help citizens exercise their rights: Websites were built, and two full-page advertisements were purchased from a major newspaper in Taiwan and in the *New York Times*.

Members of the Sunflower Movement sat in the courtyard of the Legislative Yuan building as a way to show their discontent.

Blocked Twitter Users Sue

When U.S. President Donald J. Trump blocked seven Twitter users from seeing or interacting with his account in July 2017, they sued. The lawsuit argued that the president's Twitter feed, @realDonaldTrump, which is not the official @POTUS account but the account he uses to comment about policies and current events, is an important source of information and a public forum. They argued that blocking them from seeing it is unconstitutional. The government argued that since Trump's account is his own personal account rather than an official government account, he is allowed to block anyone he wants, as any other Twitter user would be. As of early 2018, several groups that support free speech had joined the lawsuit, but no further progress has been made. It may be several months before the court is able to hear the case.

Many of the activists of the Sunflower Movement were young; in fact, most were students. Since the movement began, there has been a greater pull for more independence from China. The CSSTA was a widely misunderstood bill, but citizens were enraged that the government seemed to be trying to slip the bill through parliament without comment. It felt like a betrayal. The occupation of parliament sparked a large anti-China demonstration. "My parents still think we are Chinese," activist Kevin Wang told the BBC. "In University I began doubting what I had been taught was correct ... Now I believe Taiwan should be independent in all ways possible."[15] Many Sunflower protesters were hoping to secure the official sovereign identity of Taiwan, and they worried that closer ties from the trade agreement would make it inevitable that Taiwan would be assimilated into larger China. The immediate result of the Sunflower Movement was that the trade agreement was not ratified, or given formal approval.

Citizen Journalism

The internet has been compared to a virtual town hall, where anyone can come and voice an opinion to other citizens and to the individuals in government. This was apparent in the Sunflower Movement, where volunteers worked together using technology to collaboratively edit documents.

Anyone with access to a device with video-recording technology has the power to share videos with people through the internet.

Anyone can add to what can be seen online. With so many people who have access to smartphones with video-recording technology, citizens are often the first to post about a crisis or a situation. Citizen journalism, or street journalism, has some real advantages: It can share an otherwise unknown perspective from a community, it can cover an event of which the mainstream media is unaware, and it can help get citizens more involved in the issues that affect their communities.

However, there are also some drawbacks to citizens' involvement in journalism. Often facts are not checked before a post goes viral, and rumors are easily spread. For instance, during Hurricane Sandy in 2012, a businessman named Sashank Tripathi purposely spread misinformation, such as his statement that all the power would be shut off in Manhattan, New York, by the power company. This created confusion and more panic than was necessary when it was picked up and spread by the media. After it became known that Tripathi had lied, he had to issue a public apology and came close to getting in legal trouble. "I love the idea of citizen journalists," Tyler Mahoney wrote for the *Huffington Post*. "I love the idea that anyone can exercise his or her voice, but this ideal works best when people understand journalistic ethics."[16] With the volume of articles that exist on the internet, it can be easy to lose track of what is real and what is not. Citizen journalists—those who are more and more on the forefront of developing news stories—need to be aware and do their best to report news accurately.

ON CITIZEN JOURNALISM

"Journalism is too important to be left to the professionals."

—Alex Steffen, editor of *Worldchanging: A User's Guide for the 21st Century*

Alex Steffen, ed., *Worldchanging: A User's Guide for the 21st Century.* New York, NY: Abrams, 2008, p. 392.

In activism, citizen journalism can be very effective. It may also be the only way a population hears about what is actually going on. For instance, when a corrupt government has authority over the national newspapers, mainstream media articles may not reflect the actual state of events but rather a version laced with propaganda, which is the deliberate spread of allegations or ideas to damage someone else's cause or further their own cause.

Media Literacy

New technologies are created every day to better connect the digital world. For example, since early June 2017, activists DeRay Mckesson and Sam Sinyangwe have used the power of a bot, with the help of the tech cooperative Feel Train, to help people remain aware and give encouragement, especially to those in the black protest community. The @StayWokeBot auto-tweets new followers with encouraging messages, and when followers tweet at it with the name of their state, the bot sends them contact information for their state's senators.

This is work that not too long ago was taken on by the activists themselves. "There's a growing understanding that this work takes a lot of time, not to mention a profound emotional and psychological toll,"[17] noted Caitlin Dewey of the *Washington Post*. Time will tell if a chatbot is successful in engaging with supporters, but new and similar technologies may make it easier to be an activist.

As education about media literacy—or the ability to evaluate, create, analyze, and access media—grows, more and more people will have the tools necessary to engage in online communities in a critical fashion. In fact, some people believe media literacy education should be a mandatory subject in young people's education. Larry Atkins, author of *Skewed: A Critical Thinker's Guide to Media Bias*, argued that media literacy can keep people from "drowning in a vast sea of competing ideas."[18]

Digital Art Activism

It has long been a practice of artists, writers, and other creative people to engage with their audiences with the goal of provoking change. One historical example is Pablo Picasso, who painted *Guernica* as a reaction to the Nazis' bombing of the town in Basque Country, Spain, from which the painting gets its name.

The Nazis did this before World War II officially broke out as a way to test their bombs. The painting shows the victims of the bombing, and it also brought attention to the suffering of civilians during the Spanish Civil War, which was taking place at the time. It has become an anti-war symbol.

Picasso's Guernica was the artist's anti-war symbol. Today, artists have an incredible reach through the internet, and many of them have created politically charged works.

With the development of technology, it is easier for creative people to share their activism campaigns. A person does not need to be an already-known artist to share a politically-inspired work. All they must do is put up a website or share a post on social media.

THE INTERNET IS FOR EVERYONE

"There's no bouncer, no gatekeeper, and no barrier to entering these scenes: You don't have to be rich, you don't have to be famous, and you don't have to have a fancy résumé or a degree from an expensive school. Online, everyone—the artist and the curator, the master and the apprentice, the expert and the amateur—has the ability to contribute something."

—Austin Kleon, artist and writer

Austin Kleon, *Show Your Work!* New York, NY: Workman Publishing Company, Inc., 2014, p. 12.

When artist Steve Lambert announced on the crowdfunding website Kickstarter that he would be putting together an art installation and documenting its progress online, he raised almost twice as much as he had hoped through donations. The total amount he raised was $16,986. His project, titled *Capitalism Works for Me!*, consists of a huge LED sign that gives people an option to vote either yes or no to the question of whether capitalism (an economic system in which resources are privately owned and the prices, distribution, and production of these goods are determined by competition) works for them. The sign traveled to several locations, starting in Cleveland, Ohio, on August 26, 2011. Other locations included Boston, Massachusetts; Los Angeles, California; the Netherlands; England; and Times Square in New York City.

As Lambert explained, it is often difficult to have conversations when people's views are so polarized, or completely opposite. His sign was an effort to start that conversation; it started with online fundraising and ended with a website. "This is what art does well," he wrote. "It creates a space where new ideas and perspectives can be explored ... Every aspect of the interaction draws them [the participants] into more complex questions and conversations, leading to new thoughts and ideas about a better world."[19]

After Lambert completed the physical aspect of his project, it found a home online. He posted interviews with people from all different walks of life who had very different answers to the question, and anyone can go to his website, Visit Steve, to learn and engage.

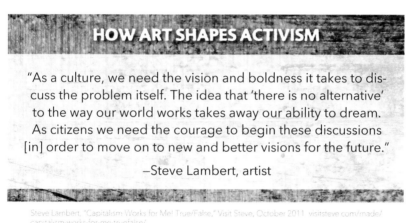

HOW ART SHAPES ACTIVISM

"As a culture, we need the vision and boldness it takes to discuss the problem itself. The idea that 'there is no alternative' to the way our world works takes away our ability to dream. As citizens we need the courage to begin these discussions [in] order to move on to new and better visions for the future."

–Steve Lambert, artist

Steve Lambert, "Capitalism Works for Me! True/False," Visit Steve, October 2011. visitsteve.com/made/capitalism-works-for-me-truefalse/

Political Division

Social media has made it easier to communicate with leaders. Many politicians have Twitter accounts, which are used to communicate about campaign issues, new legislation, and emergencies. In addition, internet users are just a message away from sending their ideas, praise, and criticisms.

When online activism is used as a tool in political and social activism campaigns, it can be very powerful. However, such a tool can also have its dark side. With information coming from everywhere, it can be difficult to figure out the truth. It can also make polarized opinions even more powerful. The internet has made the divide between the two main political parties in the United States possibly even deeper, especially in light of the fact that internet users typically see information that leans toward the beliefs they already hold.

This happens because of the way search engines collect user information and position advertisements. A newsfeed on Facebook, for example, will typically show a person information that is already in line with their beliefs and lifestyle. Businesses and political campaigns spend money to show certain ads to certain people. Pre–internet era studies have shown that it is not typical for people to speak up about their political beliefs when they think others will not agree with them. That phenomenon has been called the "spiral of silence," and it has translated to social media websites. When people believe their followers agree with a point of view, they are more likely to post about it.

Democrats and Republicans see very different social media feeds in relation to hot topics such as gun control, terrorism, and health care. The *Wall Street Journal* created a webpage to portray this phenomenon in real time. The newspaper created two different Facebook accounts, one that was very liberal and one that was very conservative. Visitors to the website can see exactly what is being said by different party lines—and the differences are staggering. The articles that appear on each side often show completely opposite points of view, which shows that when people identify with a particular party, they often no longer see the other side's point of view unless they go looking for it on other parts of the internet. The feed is pulled from sources that have at least 100 shares and that are from sources with at least 100,000 followers.

Keeping this in mind, many politicians have the ability to cater their messages to a different set of voters. One message that works for one demographic may not work for another, and with targeted ads, a politician may use different advertisements in their strategies.

The First President on Social Media

When Barack Obama was elected president in 2008, it was in no small part due to his effective campaign strategy. It was a strategy that utilized online technologies to spread the word— the first nationally successful political campaign to do so. Obama's campaign was the effort of 8 million volunteers on social networking websites. He attracted 2 million Facebook followers, and more than 100 million internet users watched his YouTube videos.

As author Jonathan Tisch noted,

The campaign raised unprecedented sums of money using the Internet. And on election day, the Obama team used text messages sent to millions of supporters to complement traditional get-out-the-vote activities—at an estimated cost of $1.56 per vote garnered, as compared with the $32 spent to produce the same vote via printed leaflets.[20]

Obama's strategy was powerful because it allowed supporters to have a more active role in the political campaign. Many people felt they truly had a stake in the outcome of the presidential race. According to Tisch, "The Obama campaign didn't merely use young volunteers, as most campaigns do. It created an innovative campaign infrastructure specifically designed by and for today's tech-happy Millennial generation, using the communication tools young people rely on and trust."[21]

The use of social media to engage with the American public and the rest of the world did not end with Obama's campaign. During his time in the White House, Obama continued to use social media to engage with the world by posting videos, tweeting, and more. Obama has been called the first social-media president.

Social Media Politics

With Donald Trump's victory and election to the office of president, it is clear that social media and the internet have helped create a new age of political candidates. During the election process and throughout his presidency, Trump has worked to engage with social media users, especially through a large volume of tweets. In fact, he has been called the first Twitter president by some.

Trump's use of the social media website has been extremely controversial. He claims that traditional media outlets report false content, or "fake news," about him, and therefore, he uses Twitter to set the record straight. On July 1, 2017, Trump tweeted, "My use of social media is not Presidential—it's MODERN DAY PRESIDENTIAL. Make America Great Again!"[22]

During the election year, 24 percent of U.S. adults used social media posts as a way of keeping up with the campaigns rather than a candidate's websites or campaign emails.

Critics of Trump point to the fact that many of his updates on Twitter are contradictory and different than official policies enacted by the White House, and some people believe that many of his comments are inappropriate for the president of the United States to make. A July 2017 poll by ABC News and the *Washington Post* revealed that 59 percent of the respondents found the President's use of the social media website questionable. For example, on November 11, 2017, he tweeted about the North Korean leader Kim Jong-un: "Why would Kim Jong-un insult me by calling me 'old,' when I would NEVER call him 'short and fat?' Oh well, I try so hard to be his friend—and maybe someday that will happen!"[23]

Supporters and critics of Trump may react to this tweet differently, but no matter where one falls on the political spectrum, it would be difficult to argue that Trump's use of social media has not had an effect on politics in the modern world.

SOCIAL MEDIA AND PRESIDENT TRUMP

"I doubt I would be here if it weren't for social media, to be honest with you."

–Donald Trump, 45th president of the United States

Quoted in Chris Baynes, "Donald Trump Says He Would Not Be President Without Twitter," *Independent*, October 22, 2017. www.independent.co.uk/news/world/americas/us-politics/donald-trump-tweets-twitter-social-media-facebook-instagram-fox-business-network-would-not-be-a8013491.html.

Some people believe the use of social media in politics is not a good thing. They argue that when the news is shrunk into social media–sized bites, it loses a lot of the complexities, which makes people less informed. Also, some argue that people's attention spans have become shorter. One study that surveyed 2,000 people and studied the brain activity of 112 other people found that the human attention span had, on average, fallen from 12 seconds to 8 seconds at the time of the mobile revolution.

Twitter's cofounder, Evan Williams, said the bigger issue "is the quality of the information we consume that is reinforcing dangerous beliefs and isolating people and limiting people's open-mindedness and respect for truth."[24] Others argue that social media posts often exploit, or use for personal gain, the emotions of individuals.

The Negative Side of Social Media Protests

Something to be aware of is that any organization may use social media to spread a message, and it is not always in a positive manner. For example, a "Unite the Right" rally organized through social media by white nationalists in Charlottesville, Virginia, in 2017 began to protest the removal of a statue of the Confederate general Robert E. Lee. Physical violence erupted when a speeding car hit a group of anti-racist protesters. Thirty-two-year-old Heather Heyer was killed, and at least 19 others were injured. The night before, protesters had rallied and marched at the University of Virginia, carrying tiki torches and yelling slogans such as "Jews will not replace us"[1] and the racist Nazi slogan "blood and soil."[2] Charlottesville's mayor, Mike Signer, condemned the march in a Facebook post, calling it a "cowardly parade of hatred, bigotry, racism, and intolerance."[3] While people are certainly allowed to meet and have an opinion about the removal of a controversial statue, this group took it much further by promoting violence and hatred.

1. Quoted in Yair Rosenberg, "'Jews Will Not Replace Us': Why White Supremacists Go After Jews," *Washington Post*, August 14, 2017. www.washingtonpost.com/news/acts-of-faith/wp/2017/08/14/jews-will-not-replace-us-why-white-supremacists-go-after-jews/?utm_term=.ce0eba54c166.
2. Quoted in Rosenberg, "'Jews Will Not Replace Us.'"
3. Mike Signer, Facebook, August 11, 2017. www.facebook.com/permalink.php?story_fbid=10155559426310629&id=51200715628.

Social Media Integrity

Certain movements have had difficulty when they disagree with the private organizations that host social media, such as Facebook. For instance, Facebook has been accused of censoring materials in relation to Kurdish residents of Turkey. Three activists said that in 2016, Facebook unfairly removed posts that did not violate the community standards. These activists—Rosa Gilbert, Mark Campbell, and Kurd Ari Murad—insisted that the social media website took down photos of a protest that accused Turkey of oppressing the Kurdish minority in the country. The Sierra Club interviewed Zeynep Tufekci, a computer programmer living in Turkey, who discovered that the problem was with Facebook's algorithms. In an attempt to control terrorist activities on social media, the algorithms actually banned everything relating to Kurdish culture because one Kurdish group has been classified as a terrorist organization by the U.S. State Department. As the Sierra Club explained, "It was as though the media decided to ban all images of shamrocks and leprechauns during the years that the Irish Republican Army was setting off bombs in London."[25]

Social media can also be used as a way to manipulate people. For example, it has been proven that during the 2016 U.S. presidential election cycle, Russia attempted to sway the opinions of U.S. voters through targeted campaigns on social media. Fake social media accounts shared websites such as DCLeaks, which posted sensitive information about prominent Americans. Facebook officials announced that there were 700 accounts that were created by a Russian company linked to the Kremlin, which is a term for the Russian government, much the same way "the White House" is used as shorthand for the American government. Additionally, $100,000 in ads were purchased to make certain issues more noticeable during the 2016 presidential campaign.

FACEBOOK IS TOO BIG FOR CHANGE

"Facebook has grown too big, and its users too complacent [comfortable], for democracy."

- Max Read, journalist

Max Read, "Does Even Mark Zuckerberg Know What Facebook Is?," New York Magazine, October 2–15, 2017. nymag.com/selectall/2017/10/does-even-mark-zuckerberg-know-what-facebook-is.html

Officials are still uncovering information and interrogating suspects as of early 2018, and more information will be needed to figure out how to move forward. As the *New York Times* explained, "Given the powerful role of social media in political contests, understanding the Russian efforts will be crucial in preventing or blunting similar, or more sophisticated, attacks in the 2018 congressional races and the 2020 presidential election."[26]

Some people believe Facebook should be required by law to disclose its advertising practices, such as how much people are paying, who is being targeted, and so on. Columbia Law School professor Tim Wu described Facebook's current advertising methods the following way: "No constraints. No regulation. No oversight. Nothing. A bunch of algorithms, basically, designed to give people what they want to hear."[27]

Chinese Online Activism

Not all people around the world experience the internet the same way. Although China has the highest number of internet users at 513 million people and online users in China spend more than 40 percent of their time on social media, Facebook has been banned by the government since 2009. Twitter and YouTube are also banned. China has strict cyber laws, which were put in place so the Communist Party could maintain control over what people see online. However, online activists in China can still use the internet to help broadcast their messages. For example, the activist organization GreatFire was started by three anonymous individuals to track the effects of the censorship system in China. The website gives users the tools to freely explore an uncensored internet, to read banned books, and to check which websites have been actively banned.

There are many questions about Facebook's role in this scandal. Critics of the social media company argue that Facebook has grown too big and that its policies are not clear. In fact, Facebook faced so much criticism after the election scandals that Mark Zuckerberg published a new mission statement, in which he wrote that Facebook would "give people the power to build community and bring the world closer together."[28] In addition, Facebook has been working to cut down on fake news stories and promote more transparent practices. During the German elections in 2017, for example, Facebook worked to shut down tens of thousands of fake accounts.

Political Crowdfunding

More recently, social media has begun to shape even more the candidates chosen to represent policy changes. It is estimated that as of early 2018, 9 percent of a political candidate's media budget was dedicated to social media in an attempt to gain the support of younger generations.

In addition, many nontraditional candidates are using the internet as a way to fund their campaigns. Websites such as Crowdpac allow individuals to fund the campaigns of candidates they would like to see in office who do not already have enough money to run. These websites allow users to donate to political causes they support. Steve Hilton, a former adviser to British Prime Minister David Cameron and a current chief executive officer (CEO), explained,

> Money underpins a huge proportion of what's wrong with politics. The need to raise money, whether that's huge amounts of money, as is needed in the U.S. to run for federal office, or even small amounts at the state level—you've got to raise money to do your campaign. And typically, that forces you to do things and say things and take positions that are not actually what you believe.[29]

Supporters of participatory politics, which involves people getting involved at all levels, think the world would be better off if the people involved in government were more diversified—meaning the more people from different backgrounds, the better. Social media and the internet help give people better access to information about political candidates, policies, and statistics—if they know where to look and how to sort through information.

CHAPTER 3

Grassroots Activism

Not all forces that change a country's political and social landscape result from the structured organization of political or social campaigns. In fact, online activism has strong beginnings in grassroots organizations, where ordinary people come together to promote a cause. In grassroots movements, social networking is a tool that connects the thoughts and opinions of many individuals. Often, one of the more important parts of social campaigns is creating a sense of solidarity in communities. Solidarity is the endgame for many social activism movements because some problems in society are either not well-known or too big to solve all at once.

Occupy Wall Street

Occupy Wall Street was a movement that had its first demonstration on September 17, 2011, in Liberty Square in Manhattan's Financial District; it ended up spreading to more than 1,500 cities worldwide. The movement began as a protest against the widening gap between the rich and the poor, the lack of accountability in regard to the financial crisis of 2008, and a sense that money ruled politics. As the organization noted, "The one thing we all have in common is that we are the 99% that will no longer tolerate the greed and corruption of the 1%."[30] These percentages refer to the top 1 percent of people in terms of wealth and the other 99 percent of people.

There was never a leader in Occupy Wall Street, and the movement insists that is because it is a leader-full movement—anyone with an idea for change would be listened to, and then the community would collectively decide what was the best route to take. In many ways, the movement functioned offline the same way as a viral movement on social media. As author and BuzzMachine blogger Jeff Jarvis noted, "Occupy Wall Street is a hashtag revolt … A Hashtag has no owner, no hierarchy, no canon or credo [motto]. It is a blank slate onto which anyone may impose his or her frustrations, complaints, demands, wishes, or principles."[31] Whether one considers the Occupy movement a success or failure probably depends on whether or not they see online activism as being effective.

The movement did not actually start on September 17, but rather a few months before that in July, when the activist group Adbusters blogged about it. According to Reuters, "The notion of Occupy Wall Street was out there but it was not gaining much attention—until, of course, it did, suddenly and with force."[32] It spread through communities by way of local tweeters. No media outlet picked up on it until the Occupy movement was in full force and hashtags such as #OccupyBoston and #OccupyDenver began trending.

Some people believe the Occupy movement was not successful because there was no clear result. However, others believe the movement helped catapult a number of issues into the national spotlight, including student debt and financial

Occupy Wall Street demonstrators, such as the ones shown here, used the internet to spread their message and organize.

inequality. Dr. Theda Skocpol believes the term "the 1 percent"—the richest Americans in the country—is very important. She said, "It's become an important way to talk about income inequality in public."[33]

The Women's March on Washington

One of the largest single-day marches in American history was the Women's March on Washington, which took place on January 21, 2017. According to the *Washington Post*, about 4.2 million people marched in the United States; the main march took place in Washington, D.C., but sister marches were held all across the country as well as around the globe. At least 261 international marches were held, with about 307,000 non-Americans participating in total. Some of the Women's March organizers also helped organize the National School Walkout, in which students across the country walked out of their schools for 17 minutes on March 14, 2018, to remember the 17 students killed in the shooting at Marjory Stoneman Douglas High School and to raise awareness about gun control.

The women's march started with Teresa Shook, a woman living in Hawai'i. The night Trump won the 2016 election, she created a Facebook event page for a march on Washington. Overnight, the page earned 10,000 responses. Various other people created their own Facebook events, and eventually, they were consolidated into one national movement, led by social activists Tamika Mallory, Carmen Perez, and Linda Sarsour.

Erica Chenoweth and Jeremy Pressman of the *Washington Post* noted that although the march was inspiring to many, there was more work to be done:

> We don't want to overestimate the power of a single march, however large. A march won't have much effect unless it's translated into continuing organized and disciplined mobilization, pressure on the government, collaborative problem-solving and electoral action. But if a march inspires, convenes and energizes, it can catalyze a great deal of change.[1]

1. Erica Chenoweth and Jeremy Pressman, "This Is What We Learned by Counting the Women's Marches," *Washington Post*, February 7, 2017. www.washingtonpost.com/news/monkey-cage/wp/2017/02/07/this-is-what-we-learned-by-counting-the-womens-marches/?utm_term=.e61d1ccc00ab.

#MeToo and #NeverAgain

While the social media campaign for the hashtag movement #MeToo went viral in October 2017, its roots started much earlier than that. Activist Tarana Burke was a youth camp director in 1996 when a young girl asked to speak to her. The girl began to tell Burke of sexual misconduct done to her by her stepfather. Burke was unable to help: She sent the girl to another counselor. "I watched her walk away from me as she tried to recapture her secrets and tuck them back into their hiding place," Burke wrote. "I watched her put her mask back on and go back into the world like she was all alone and I couldn't even bring myself to whisper … me too."[34]

Today, Burke is the senior director for the Brooklyn-based organization Girls for Gender Equity. She wrote about her experience and described what she called the Me Too movement on the website for Just Be, Inc., a youth organization that focuses on the health of young women of color, long before it became a hashtag that took the world by storm. The hashtag #MeToo ultimately went viral in 2017 when actress Alyssa Milano retweeted a call-out to victims to post in order that "we might give people a sense of the magnitude of the problem."[35]

In just two days, the hashtag was used 825,000 times on Twitter. On Facebook, 4.7 million people around the world joined in on the conversation with more than 12 million posts, comments, and reactions. Posts from around the world detailed sexual harassment experiences—unwanted sexual comments, threats, advances, or suggestions toward another person—from a diverse crowd of people.

However, it is important to note that just because someone has not posted about it on social media does not mean they are not a victim of sexual harassment. Some people choose not to participate in viral movements even if they have a shared experience, either because they disagree with it or simply do not care enough to join in. It is also important to remember that sometimes movements like these can be triggering for the people who have been victims, making them relive their traumatic experience. For some, staying out of the movement is a way to take care of their own mental health.

"Uncovering the colossal scale of the problem is revolutionary in its own right,"[36] Sophie Gilbert wrote in *The Atlantic*. The hashtag movement went viral following sexual assault and harassment accusations against movie mogul Harvey Weinstein. In the few months afterwards, many women came forward to accuse male celebrities and politicians of abusing their positions of power by sexually harassing or sexually assaulting others (engaging in illegal sexual contact which involves force upon a person who does not give consent or is unable to give consent, or which involves a person in a position of authority). It could be argued that the solidarity and popularity of #MeToo helped spur many of the victims to bravely come forward.

The awareness created by #MeToo was translated into action when some celebrities created the Time's Up movement in direct response to the original hashtag. Time's Up aims to use celebrities' visibility to create awareness of sexual harassment in workplaces where women are less able to make themselves heard, as well as to raise money for those victims who need it for legal defense in sexual harassment cases. The movement began with an open letter that was published online and signed by 400 women who work in the entertainment industry, including Reese Witherspoon, Oprah Winfrey, and Shonda Rhimes, and as of March 2018, it had raised $20 million.

Another movement that started with a hashtag is the #NeverAgain movement, which began after a shooting at Marjory Stoneman Douglas High School in Parkland, Florida, on February 14, 2018. School shootings have been in American news for some time now, but after this one, the survivors—led by students such as Emma González and David Hogg—decided to take action. Along with a group called Everytown for Gun Safety, the students organized a march on Washington, D.C. The march, which was intended to encourage lawmakers to pass common-sense gun control laws, was called the March for Our Lives and took place on March 24, 2018. The organizers received donations from celebrities such as Amal and George Clooney to make their march happen, and others called attention to the movement by posting about it on social media. Hundreds of solidarity marches were planned as well. Many people applauded the fact that the students took action rather than limiting their participation to social media, as so many people—both young and old—had done after previous shootings. Supporters of the #NeverAgain movement hope the march and other actions by the students, such as an online petition, will result in meaningful change to the gun laws in the United States.

Black Lives Matter

One of the most effective social media campaigns in history is the Black Lives Matter (BLM) movement. The United States has a long history of racism, which to this day continues to be a sensitive topic. According to a Pew Research Center survey from June 2016, 88 percent of black people say the United States needs to make changes for black people to have equal rights with white people. This research also found that people of different races see the problem differently: Only 53 percent of white people agreed.

BLM has created some real change; for instance, many cities have adopted police conduct reforms, including requiring body cameras to be worn, training officers in de-escalation tactics,

Police Kill a Disproportionate Number of Black People

U.S. population

Black   Hispanic   White

| 13% | 17% | 63% |

all people killed by police

| 31% | 12% | 52% |

people killed by police while not attacking

| 39% | 12% | 46% |

When police killings are broken down by race, it is clear that black people are killed at disproportionate rates to white people, as this information from Vox (based on analysis of FBI data) shows.

and creating independent review boards. However, not all social media movements achieve this kind of success. Although there is a Native Lives Matter movement that attempts to raise awareness of police brutality against Native Americans—who are more likely even than black people to be killed by police, according to statistics from the Center on Juvenile and Criminal Justice—it has not gained the same kind of recognition as BLM.

Police Shootings

On the night of February 26, 2012, unarmed teenager Trayvon Martin was fatally shot in a gated community in Sanford, Florida, by neighborhood watch volunteer George Zimmerman. When Zimmerman called 911 to report "a real suspicious guy"[37] in the neighborhood, he was told to stay in his SUV and not approach the person. When he disobeyed, things quickly spiraled out of control. A few minutes later, neighbors in the area reported hearing gunfire. By 7:30 p.m., Martin was pronounced dead. Zimmerman stated that he was attacked by Martin. Because there was no evidence to suggest that Zimmerman was not acting in self-defense, local police allowed him to go home; Zimmerman was not arrested.

The national news picked up on the story, and many people across the United States demanded that Zimmerman be arrested and charged with murder. Many people believed Martin was shot because of racial profiling.

A protester is shown here carrying a sign with a photo of Trayvon Martin, who was fatally shot on February 26, 2012. The reaction to Martin's shooting and other similar shootings was the foundation of Black Lives Matter (BLM).

An online petition was created by Kevin Cunningham on Change.org after reading about Martin's murder. A few days later, Cunningham was contacted by the website for approval to transfer control of the petition to Martin's family. The petition received more than 2 million supporters. Zimmerman stayed out of the public eye except to launch a low-budget website to fund-raise for his legal defense. Eventually, he was arrested, but at the trial, he was found not guilty of murder.

Wesley Lowery, a reporter who has covered many police shootings since 2012 and who wrote the book *"They Can't Kill Us All": The Story of the Struggle for Black Lives*, explained how the events of 2012 changed the reality for many black people. He wrote,

> The year 2012 was a major awakening point not just for me but also for other young black men and women across the country. We watched the Trayvon Martin shooting play out in real time on our Facebook pages and television screens. At the same time, the stories of Jordan Davis and Oscar Grant (a 2009 police shooting that was depicted in the film Fruitvale Station) solidified the undeniable feeling in our hearts that their deaths and those of other young black men were not isolated.[38]

It was after Zimmerman was pronounced not guilty that Oakland, California, activist Alicia Garza, who was 31 years old at the time, wrote a Facebook post called "a love note to black people."[39]

PART OF ALICIA GARZA'S LOVE NOTE

"[T]he sad part is, there's a section of America who is cheering and celebrating right now, and that makes me sick to my stomach. we GOTTA get it together y'all ... stop saying we are not surprised. that's a damn shame in itself. I continue to be surprised at how little Black lives matter. And I will continue that. stop giving up on black life. black people. I love you. I love us. Our lives matter."

—Alicia Garza, activist and cofounder of Black Lives Matter

Quoted in Wesley Lowery, "They Can't Kill Us All": The Story of the Struggle for Black Lives. New York, NY: Hachette Book Group, 2016, p. 87.

It was not until two years later, in 2014, that the hashtag #BlackLivesMatter went viral, after another police shooting—this time in Ferguson, Missouri. Michael Brown was fatally shot on August 9, 2014, by police officer Darren Wilson after a 911 call was made from the local grocery store. While there is doubt about what actually happened, most people agree that Brown robbed the store and Wilson was responding to the call, although Wilson later said that he confronted Michael Brown and his friend Dorian Johnson because they were walking down the middle of the street and blocking traffic. There was a scuffle, and by the end of it, Brown was shot at least six times. His body was left in the street for four hours. Wilson's defense stated that Brown attacked him and that they struggled for the gun. Johnson's story is that Brown was running away and had raised his arms in a gesture of surrender, which was ignored by Wilson.

The report of Brown's death did not come first from journalists. Emanuel Freeman, a rapper who goes by the stage name Thee Pharoah, lived in the Canfield Green apartment complex near where the incident took place. He heard the first gunshot and raced to the window with his phone in his hand. At 10:03 a.m., he tweeted, "I JUST SAW SOMEONE DIE … the police just shot someone dead in front of my crib yo."[40] To someone asking for more information, he responded: "no reason! He was running!"[41] He then posted an image of Wilson standing over the body.

While the details of the event are still disputed, what is certain is that the community responded with outrage. The day after the shooting, protests and riots flooded the streets. Many in the black community called for Wilson to be charged with murder. After Wilson was cleared of the charges in November of that year, more riots began and quickly turned violent. An angry mob destroyed businesses and burned a line of cars. A QuickTrip gas station was set on fire and burned to the ground.

At first, the protesters in Ferguson were considered to be the majority of BLM members until reporters began to realize that the movement was growing and separate from Ferguson. As of January 2017, #BlackLivesMatter had been used more than 27 million times, and that number keeps increasing as time goes on.

CALLING FOR AN END TO INSTITUTIONALIZED RACISM

"Black America is in a state of protest. The 21st-century civil rights movement, exemplified by the action taken by Garza and those like her ... is fuelled by grief and fury, by righteous rage against injustice and institutionalised racism and by frustration at the endemic [common] brutality of the state against those it deems unworthy."

–Elizabeth Day, journalist

Elizabeth Day, "#BlackLivesMatter: The Birth of a New Civil Rights Movement," *The Guardian*, July 19, 2015. www.theguardian.com/world/2015/jul/19/blacklivesmatter-birth-civil-rights-movement.

Following Black Lives Matter

Responses to BLM have taken many different forms. While some support BLM and its attempt to raise awareness of a problem that has affected the black community for decades, others see members of the group as troublemakers. A counter-movement called Blue Lives Matter was created to help police officers and their families, especially those who have been killed in the line of duty. Another goal of the organization is to counter media reports that have an anti-police bias. This group has helped introduce at least 32 bills proposing that law enforcement be included in hate crime protections. Louisiana was the first state to bring this into effect with its Blue Lives Matter bill. Opponents to this counter-movement argue that the legislation works to protect an already protected class. One Louisiana police chief noted that it could be interpreted to apply to people who are resisting arrest, which made many people nervous. In some cases, it is obvious when someone is resisting arrest, such as when someone tries to punch or otherwise physically assault a police officer to try to get away from them. However, other cases are left up to the officer's judgment, and if an officer interprets a person's movement as aggressive when it was not intended to be, that person could find themselves facing a harsh hate crime penalty for something they did accidentally.

All Lives Matter is another counter-movement. Many advocates responded to #BlackLivesMatter with the phrase #AllLivesMatter. While the idea that all lives matter is correct, saying it in response to #BlackLivesMatter misses the point. Black people in the United States have not been treated equally, historically and today. When someone says "All Lives Matter," that person is minimizing the difficulties black people have faced and continue to face in the present day.

Social media has had a major role in bringing these issues to the forefront of social consciousness. As a moral awareness campaign, BLM has forced policy makers to choose sides, and individuals on social media continue to weigh in on the conversation.

For example, a blog on Tumblr called *If They Gunned Me Down* calls into question the photos used after shootings, which often depict black victims in a threatening or unflattering way. On this blog, participants post two

A BLM protester is shown here holding a sign that explains why it is inappropriate to respond to #BlackLivesMatter with #AllLivesMatter.

pictures of themselves side by side as they ask which picture the media would use if they were gunned down. One of these photos is typically the individual smiling, often well-dressed and looking successful, and the other represents a more unflattering view—for instance, someone looking angry, wearing clothing with swear words on it, or drinking alcohol. The pictures call attention to the fact that everyone has multiple sides to their personality and that just because someone looks a certain way in one picture, it does not mean they act that way all the time. The social media response has called into question the way traditional media sources present a story.

CHAPTER 4

Hacktivism and Slacktivism

Hackers find and utilize weaknesses in computer systems. This can be legal or illegal, depending on the situation. Often governments and companies hire hackers to find the weaknesses in their systems so they can improve them. Other hackers use their skills without permission, which is illegal.

Hacktivism is the blending of hacking and activism. Most hacktivists use their skills to fight injustices in the digital world, although they generally do so in illegal ways. These individuals see their illegal activity as being for a greater good. Others disagree, but hacktivists have made their impact on society since the dawn of the internet.

Anonymous

"Today, thanks to our current technology, the civil rights movement has spread to the internet and across the globe,"[42] said a person wearing a Guy Fawkes mask in a video on the official Anonymous website. The hacktivist group Anonymous, which originated in 2003, has been linked to many high-profile hacking incidents.

Anonymous is faceless and leaderless: Anyone can join the group just by deciding to be part of it. Because of the amorphous, or unclear, nature of Anonymous, its goals are not specific. Rather, there is a loose goal to promote freedom of speech and limit censorship from governments and organizations.

One example of a hack done by Anonymous was against the militant terrorist group the Islamic State of Iraq and Syria (ISIS), after *Charlie Hebdo*, a French magazine, was attacked for running several cartoons featuring the Islamic prophet Muhammad.

According to Islamic law, Muhammad should never be shown in a picture, statue, or any other visual representation. Although it was offensive to some Muslims to see a picture of Muhammad in a magazine, most voiced their opposition through peaceful protests. However, two people who claimed to be part of ISIS took things to the extreme by entering the *Charlie Hebdo* offices in 2015 and shooting the employees, killing 12. Anonymous released a video on YouTube saying its members would be "fighting in memory of those innocent people who fought for freedom of expression,"[43] meaning the employees of *Charlie Hebdo*. Anonymous was declaring war on ISIS, and it successfully took down 20,000 Twitter accounts that were used by ISIS for recruitment and propaganda.

Anonymous has also come off the screen: At protests around the world, people have started to wear the iconic Guy Fawkes mask. These masks became the symbol of Anonymous after the graphic novel and movie *V for Vendetta* showed the main character, V—a freedom fighter in a futuristic version of Great Britain—wearing one. The mask used in the graphic novel and movie is styled after Guy Fawkes, who was a ringleader in the Gunpowder Plot, the goal of which was to blow up the Houses of Parliament in London, England in the early 1600s.

The global hacktivist group Anonymous is leaderless, but members of the group are often associated with the Guy Fawkes mask.

Steubenville

In 2013, two athletes, Ma'Lik Richmond and Trent Mays, from Steubenville, Ohio, were tried and convicted of raping a 16-year-old girl in 2012. Also indicted were the city's school superintendent, Michael McVey—who was charged with tampering with evidence and obstructing justice—and an elementary school principal and two coaches, charged with failing to report child abuse and making false statements.

A blurred Instagram photo of the victim was shared on social media and went viral. That picture, taken by her ex-boyfriend, was used as evidence in the case, and it shows the victim unconscious and being carried by someone. In addition, other teens shared videos and comments on social media about the incident, which played a role in the judgment.

More and more, social media posts and other digital records are being used as evidence in the courtroom. For example, in this case, Mays admitted via text that he had committed acts against the victim that are legally considered sexual assault. "You were your own accuser, through the social media that you chose to publish your criminal conduct on,"[44] said the victim's mother to the two teenage boys.

In 2017, 29-year-old Deric Lostutter was sentenced to two years in federal prison in connection with the case, but Lostutter's involvement was very different. As the Anonymous member KYAnonymous, Lostutter had led a movement that catapulted the rape and cover-up case into national news outlets. After posting an Op (short for "operation") video, which is a manifesto against a specific target, Lostutter inspired someone else to hack into the Steubenville booster club website as well as the personal email of the webmaster, Jim Parks. The hacker posted Lostutter's Op as the front page of the website. In the Op, Lostutter claimed that Anonymous had the information of all the people involved in the cover-up, which would be posted online for the world to see unless all accused parties came forward and issued a public apology to the victim and her family before New Year's Day. "Our goal wasn't to hack," Lostutter told David Kushner of *Rolling Stone magazine*. "Our goal was to get the attention of higher authorities to get involved in Steubenville."[45]

Using Twitter and YouTube, Lostutter followed what was happening in Steubenville. In addition, he organized two rallies using his Anonymous name. People in Guy Fawkes masks showed up to the rallies.

On January 2, 2013, Lostutter uploaded a video he had received from a mysterious person on Twitter, where Michael Nodianos, a former Steubenville athlete, joked about the rape the day it occurred. Later this same day, a website called LocalLeaks released what it called *The Steubenville Files*, accusing prominent members of the town of various crimes. According to some, a lot of what was said was false. Some protesters began to get violent, throwing rocks at the homes of some locals. Lostutter took to the web to say that the violence was not endorsed by Anonymous, but once something is out on the internet, it is very hard for the original poster to control.

All of this came back to Lostutter. Even other members of Anonymous were not backing the movement any longer, as they were angered by the attentioned placed on KYAnonymous, which went against the idea that they were a leaderless, faceless organization. On April 17, a Special Weapons and Tactics (SWAT) team stormed Lostutter's house. They were looking for evidence that Lostutter had hacked Jim Parks.

After this, Lostutter posted to the website ProjectKnightSec. In this message, he named himself. He had supporters; 400,000 signatures were gathered in his defense to be handed to the Ohio Attorney General. Nita Chaudhary, the cofounder of women's rights group UltraViolet, said, "This is rape culture at work. Deric helped expose a horrible crime and cover-up, and he is facing five times more jail time than the rapists? It's disgusting and it's a wake up call for our entire nation."[46] However, Lostutter's opponents believe he went too far.

Leaking Data

Another type of hacktivism is called leaktivism, which is when a person or an activist organization acquires and shares information that does not belong to them. The idea behind leaktivism is that leaking truthful information is effective social protest.

Founded in 2006, WikiLeaks is a media organization and library that publishes restricted information. The nonprofit organization has released more than 10 million secret documents to the public, including tens of thousands of documents relating to the wars in Afghanistan and Iraq that were acquired by U.S. Army intelligence analyst Bradley Manning, a trans woman who now goes by the name Chelsea Manning. In one of the acquired videos, which WikiLeaks titled "Collateral Murder," U.S. military personnel are shown killing more than a dozen people—including two staff members of the news website Reuters—in New Baghdad, an Iraqi suburb.

Julian Assange, an Australian computer programmer, is the editor-in-chief and spokesperson for Wikileaks. He is an online activist, and people have strong feelings about his work and his personality. Feelings about Assange and WikiLeaks have only intensified as the years pass. Many early supporters of WikiLeaks called the motives of Assange and his colleagues into question when, before the 2016 presidential election, WikiLeaks released emails from Hillary Clinton's private account. Assange received further criticism when he was faced with two charges of sexual assault (which have since been dropped). However, others see Assange's work as fundamental. According to journalist Raffi Khatchadourian, "Assange has become a quixotic [unrealistic] cultural icon, helping to give the solitary act of whistleblowing the contours of a movement."[47]

In 2010, Assange was arrested in London after Sweden issued an international arrest warrant for him for the sexual assault charges, which Assange has repeatedly denied. He was under house arrest for two years. In 2012, Assange entered the Ecuadorian Embassy in London, and as of early 2018, he has not left the building since then, as the British government has promised to arrest him and take him to court as an international criminal if he does so. Embassies are considered to be on foreign soil, so the British government cannot enter the building to arrest him. Despite pressure from international communities for WikiLeaks to refrain from making comments on specific world events, Assange has continued to comment. In 2016, the Ecuadorian government decided to temporarily shut down Assange's internet access so Ecuador would not be seen as interfering in the affairs of other governments. In 2017, when Catalonia attempted a referendum that would allow citizens to vote for a move for independence from Spain, the Ecuadorian government asked Assange not to comment on the situation since it involved relations with friendly countries. Assange refused to stay silent, and he encouraged the independence movement.

Other leaks have involved the United States as well, including leaks concerning government surveillance. On June 6, 2013,

Shown here is the Ecuadorian Embassy in London, where WikiLeaks spokesperson Julian Assange has been living since 2012.

the first newspaper article hit. This article, written by Glenn Greenwald for the British newspaper the *Guardian*, revealed a top secret court order that allowed the National Security Agency (NSA) to collect Verizon users' telephone records, regardless of whether or not they were suspected of a crime. More articles followed: The next day, the *Guardian* and the *Washington Post* published articles about PRISM, a top-secret program that allowed the U.S. intelligence community to gain information from nine internet companies, which focused on e-mail and stored data.

On June 9, 2013, it was revealed that the source of the NSA leaks was Edward Snowden, a young man who was contracted to work at an NSA facility through the company Booz Allen Hamilton. During his employment, Snowden collected information about the intelligence practices of the U.S. government. On June 14, 2013, the U.S. Justice Department charged Snowden with theft of national defense information. Snowden boarded a plane from Hong Kong, China, that was supposed to land in Ecuador, but which stalled in Russia. Snowden stayed in the airport's transit center for a month, unsure of what would happen if he left. Meanwhile, more documents continued to come to light, which also brought into question some practices of British authorities.

Snowden has been given permission to stay in Russia through 2020 and may be allowed to apply for Russian citizenship. Critics of Snowden think that perhaps he provided key government and military information to Russia in exchange for a safe place to stay. Supporters of Snowden created a petition on the official We the People website in 2015, where they stated, "Edward Snowden is a national hero and should be immediately issued a full, free, and absolute pardon for any crimes he has committed or may have committed related to blowing the whistle on secret NSA surveillance programs."[48] The petition gained more than 160,000 signatures, which prompted a response by the Obama administration. Lisa Monaco, Obama's adviser on homeland security and counterterrorism, responded by saying, "He should come home to the United States, and be judged by a jury of his peers—not hide behind the cover of an authoritarian regime. Right now, he's running away from the consequences of his actions."[49]

Edward Snowden spoke via video at the launch of a campaign that was meant to convince President Obama to pardon him.

Taking leaktivism even further, the Panama Papers were released in 2016 by the International Consortium of Investigative Journalists (ICIJ) after an anonymous source gave them to the German newspaper *Süddeutsche Zeitung*. The 11.5 million documents were leaked from the database of the world's fourth largest offshore law firm, Mossack Fonesca. This is the biggest leak in history as of 2018, and the documents reveal some of the ways the rich can exploit offshore shell companies to keep business dealings secret, to stay rich, and to prevent paying taxes. As the financial website SmartAsset explained,

> A shell company is a business that's meant to hold funds and manage another entity's financial transactions. Unlike traditional companies, shell corporations don't hire employees. They aren't traded on exchanges and they neither make money nor provide customers with products or services ...
>
> In most parts of the wold, shell companies are considered to be perfectly legal entities ... But as was the case with the Panama Papers leak—which reportedly revealed the use of 214,000 shell companies—these corporations sometimes operate as illegal vehicles ...
>
> Shell companies are often set up to mask the identity of whoever stashes their assets within them ...
>
> Occasionally, companies take advantage of the secretive nature of shell companies by participating in illegitimate activities like money laundering [to disguise the source of illegally obtained money by making it appear as though it came from a legimate source]. Reportedly, that's just one of the crimes that the individuals involved in the Panama Papers scandal committed.[50]

In November 2017, even more documents were released, called the Paradise Papers.

According to reporter Jake Bernstein, "this global elite lives by this very different set of rules than the rest of us." He noted that the United States loses roughly $70 billion per year due to corporations moving taxes to these offshore accounts. "That's money that could go to schools, that could go to infrastructure. [It] could go to police. It could go to health care. But it's not. Instead, it's disappearing in the Caymans or the Bahamas or Bermuda or places like that."[51]

Exposing corruption is not without its dangers. In October 2017, the Maltese investigative journalist Daphne Caruana Galizia, who led the Panama Papers investigation, was murdered when her car was bombed near her home. Whistleblowers are also facing more serious penalties from governments: For example, the U.S. Defense Department created an "Insider Threat" program that puts personnel under continuous evaluation.

Shown here is a message that was left at a candlelight vigil for journalist Daphne Caruana Galizia, who was killed in a car bombing after reporting on high-profile cases such as the Panama Papers.

Net Neutrality

Net neutrality is the idea that companies that control content on the internet cannot alter the way consumers see data. It ensures that internet users have the ability to communicate freely online and that certain websites are not blocked or slowed down. Net neutrality is an important concept when it comes to protecting free speech on the internet as well as protecting the First Amendment, which states that Congress cannot prohibit freedom of religion, speech, the press, or the right to peaceably assemble.

In 2015, the Federal Communications Commission (FCC) released an Open Internet Order that laid down legal guidelines that would ensure an open internet; however, in November 2017, FCC chairman Ajit Pai outlined a plan that would limit government oversight and get rid of net neutrality. Many petitions circulated the internet, yet in December 2017, net neutrality was repealed despite the public's lack of support for this move. Most companies have promised not to interfere with internet speeds when their competitors' websites or services are involved, but if they change their minds later, their decision to do so will be legal. Examples such as this make it clear that it is important for online activists to remain aware of their digital rights.

After FCC chairman Ajit Pai outlined changes to the laws on net neutrality, protests were held across the country, often in front of service providers' offices.

MOCKING SLACKTIVISM IN THE EGYPTIAN UPRISINGS

"I don't understand how the people of Tunisia overthrew their government without me signing an e-petition or changing my Twitter avatar."

—Twitter user amuchmoreexotic

Quoted in Nadia Idle and Alex Nunns, eds., *Tweets from Tahrir: Egypt's Revolution as it Unfolded, in the Words of the People Who Made It.* New York, NY: OR Books, 2011, p. 27.

Slacktivism

Internet users are often bombarded with campaigns designed to be shared. That is the point of social media, and most campaigns are built with that goal in mind. However, that ease of information sometimes makes it a little too easy to become involved—often at the expense of knowledge of the deeper issues at play.

Activism by sharing a hashtag or by signing an online petition has been called slacktivism or armchair activism. Digital Trends describes slacktivism as "any time you endorse a cause on social media or sign an online petition without taking any corollary action outside the digital world."[52]

By this definition, sharing a post or signing an e-petition is engaging in slacktivism. Some argue that these actions have a value in the real world, while others argue that slacktivism, which does a lot to falsely convince a person that they have done something for the broader world, does not support the causes they champion, and sometimes it even hurts them.

HASHTAGS ARE NOT ACTIVISM

"A hashtag is not a movement. A hashtag does not make you Dr. King. A hashtag does not change anything. It's a hashtag. It's you, sitting on your butt, typing into your computer and then going back to binge-watching your favorite show."

—Shonda Rhimes, television producer and screenwriter

Quoted in Erin Lee, "How Effective is Social Media Activism?," *The Dartmouth,* February 12, 2016. www.thedartmouth.com/article/2016/02/how-effective-is-social-media-activism/

Many critics of online activism consider it to be ineffective in the grand scheme of things. These individuals worry that online activism does not translate to action, but rather is an illusion of taking steps toward a desired outcome. In this worldview, a click is just a click and a post is just a post.

UK Government and Parliament

Petition

Prevent Donald Trump from making a State Visit to the United Kingdom.

Donald Trump should be allowed to enter the UK in his capacity as head of the US Government, but he should not be invited to make an official State Visit because it would cause embarrassment to Her Majesty the Queen.

▶ More details

Sign this petition

1,099,018 signatures

One of the biggest online petitions in Britain in 2016 and 2017, shown here, made no impact on government decisions.

The Monetary Argument

Considering how long it takes to establish a campaign on social media, some argue that nonprofit organizations never see the return on their investment. According to a 2014 Pew Research Center survey, the average number of Facebook friends a person has is 338, and 15 percent of Facebook users have more than 500 friends, so it would be easy to assume that a person would have many chances to influence others. However, this may not be the case.

First, much of what a person sees on social media is skewed to match their personal preferences. Data collection has resulted in some accurate results about people online; for instance, an algorithm developed by a Cambridge psychology professor has the ability to use Facebook likes to accurately describe personality. By analyzing just 10 likes, the algorithm could evaluate a person's character better than their coworker could, on average. By analyzing 70 likes, the algorithm could evaluate a person's character better than their friends could. This shows that algorithms can easily be used to show people things they already like. The benefit to social media websites is that people will be more likely to use the website when they see things they like, which will allow them to make more money by selling advertising space on their website. However, the drawback in terms of social connection and activism is that people are less likely to encounter a different point of view. This has led some experts to express concerns about social media websites becoming "echo chambers," or situations in which a person sees the ideas they already believe in reinforced over and over again, without ever seeing the opposing point of view. An echo chamber can decrease discussion and the exchange of differing views.

Second, most people who like a page or share an event do not follow through outside of the internet—whether that means donating to the cause or showing up in person to contribute time and energy. A study published in the *Journal of Sociological Science* studied the Save Darfur page, one of the largest causes on Facebook. Of the more than 1 million people who signed up for the page, less than 3,000 donated money to the cause.

The opinion of the authors of the study was that the page gave the "illusion of activism."[53] Similarly, after a national disaster such as a large-scale terrorist attack, many people change their profile picture to show the colors of the flag of the nation affected. They may also create a post about how they are sending their "thoughts and prayers" to the victims. This does not create any kind of change, but many people feel as though they are doing something by showing support—in fact, many feel it is the only thing they are able to do, and some people appreciate the gesture. However, others have condemned these moves as self-congratulatory, especially when they are not followed up with meaningful action; as college student Andrea Vale wrote on the *USA Today* blog in 2015, "There are those who post political opinions to portray an image as a sophisticated activist, yet who would never pick up a picket sign unless someone was there to photograph them doing it."[54]

In January 2010, some people made posts on Facebook that named a color without any other context or explanation. Many women received a private message similar to this:

> *Something fun is going on. Write the color of your bra in your status. Just the color, nothing else. And send this on to ONLY women no men. It will be neat to see if this will spread the wings of cancer awareness. It will be fun to see how long it takes before the men wonder why the women have a color in their status ... LOL!*[55]

The origin of the message is unknown, but it quickly spread across the internet. Supporters of the campaign believe any publicity is good publicity. Andrea Rader of the Susan G. Komen Foundation told ABC News, "We think it's terrific ... It's a terrific example of how little things get started on the Internet and go a long way to raise cancer awareness."[56] All About Facebook called the campaign "a fast, free and fun way for women to raise awareness about breast cancer and remind other women to get themselves examined."[57]

Critics of the Bra Color Campaign are quick to point out, though, that these posts were not related to or associated with any kind of awareness campaign or research-based organization. Many say these posts were created as a joke, and they also criticize the fact that there was no direct call to action to raise money or to get cancer screenings.

Suckerism

It can be very easy to believe an internet hoax, or trick, without thinking about it. Many internet campaigns are designed to shock and pull on the heartstrings. However, when someone shares a post that is factually inaccurate but quick to draw emotion, that is what Digital Trends has coined "suckerism."[1] For example, in 1989, a young boy with cancer named Craig Shergold wanted to get into the *Guinness Book of World Records* for receiving the largest number of greeting cards. By 1991, he had received 33 million cards. Shergold eventually recovered from his cancer, and the Make-A-Wish Foundation requested multiple times for people to stop sending the cards even though the organization was never involved to begin with; however, the cards still keep coming. His original request was not a hoax, but this post is still often shared even though Shergold no longer wants the cards. Since then, a number of hoaxes in the same vein have gone around—and in one case, a family had to move because the amount of mail they were receiving was too much for them to handle.

Because it is human instinct to want to help those in need, these kinds of campaigns can be very effective. It is up to people online to fact-check campaigns. One resource that can be very helpful is Snopes, which has become the largest fact-checking website on the internet.

1. Kate Knibbs, "Slacktivists, Unite! Social Media Campaigns Aren't Just Feel-Good Back Patting," Digital Trends, May 15, 2013. www.digitaltrends.com/opinion/slacktivists-unite-social-media-campaigns-arent-just-feel-good-back-patting/.

In fact, some people's critiques go even further. Writer Hortense Smith, for example, is critical of the fact that the campaign urged women to be sexy and hold knowledge over the heads of men, as though breast cancer does not affect all sexes. Smith wrote,

If anything, the constant sexualization of and cutesy-poo approach to breast cancer pushes people to take it less seriously … Perhaps

it's time we all recognize that awareness alone is not enough; posting your bra color may have temporarily reminded someone that breast cancer exists, but it certainly didn't do anything to ensure that it won't exist forever.[58]

The Dakota Access Pipeline

On October 24, 2016, more than 1 million people from all over the world used the Facebook check-in feature to say they were at the Standing Rock Reservation in North Dakota. They were not physically present; instead, their check-ins were a sign of solidarity and a way for people to help the protesters, who consisted of members of more than 90 Native American nations as well as people who were not Native American. The protesters were assembled to halt the building of the Dakota Access Pipeline (DAPL), which was to be built to send crude oil from Lake Oahe, a water source for Native Americans, to Illinois. The pipeline cost $3.8 billion. Native Americans and environmentalists worried the pipeline would pollute water and destroy sacred sites. At the protest's peak, more than 10,000 protesters set up tents at Oceti Sakowin Camp, and hundreds of them were arrested. It was the biggest Native American protest since the 1970s.

One of the viral posts calling Facebook users to join in said that check-ins were used to overwhelm and confuse the police. It claimed the Morton County Sheriff's Department had been using Facebook's check-in feature to target protesters. Many of the posts were accompanied by the message "DO NOT SHARE, COPY AND PASTE THIS,"[59] since some people's privacy settings prevent shared posts from being seen. Some messages encouraged protesters to check in privately with the directions and then publicly without the directions, in order to keep their actions secret from the police. What was true of all the posts is that their source is not known. The Sacred Stone camp acknowledged that it did not come from them.

However, this campaign did not have the intended effect. It turned out the police were not monitoring Facebook for protesters, at least not according to a statement issued by the Morton County Sheriff's Department. As Madison Malone Kircher noted,

Even if you don't believe the sheriff, it's worth considering exactly what the Facebook status is claiming. What would be the point of the cops monitoring Facebook to see voluntary check-ins? Anyone who wants to avoid the sheriff simply wouldn't check in on Facebook. Plus: The Sheriff's Department already knows exactly where the protesters are located.[60]

Whether or not the check-in setup was a hoax, it was still followed by more than 1 million people taking social media action. The effectiveness of this online action is debatable. Supporters of social media activism argue that the national attention to the area brought a large wave of public support, and it also put the spotlight on a number of issues faced by Native Americans, such as high unemployment and poverty rates. The media coverage of the protest before the social media check-in was minimal.

The Sacred Stone Camp thanked everyone for the support, saying, "We appreciate a diversity of tactics and encourage people to come up with creative ways to act in solidarity, both online and as real physical allies." Continuing in the statement emailed to *Mic*, they wrote,

We would like to see these thousands of people take physical action to demand that their bank divest, their police forces withdraw, and the Army Corps and Obama administration halt the construction of this pipeline. We would like CitiBank, Bank of Tokyo and Mizho Bank to cancel their pending $1.1 billion dollar loan to DAPL. We'd also like to see people connect with indigenous and environmental struggles in their own bioregion. We'd like you to investigate and organize around your personal relationship to fossil fuel consumption and colonization …

We also need 10,000 to 100,000 people to join us here on the ground. Now.[61]

Supporters also say the check-in was never meant to solve the problem, but it was a tool in the arsenal of activists as they sought to make the issues known.

Critics of social media activism argue that social media was quick to forget about the protesters, especially in light of the approval Trump gave to finishing the pipeline in early 2017. There was an effort to rally against the approval of the pipeline by environmental organizations such as the Sierra Club, and there was a petition circulated by the Democratic National Committee to fight climate change. However, as writer Emily Dreyfuss argued, "the whiplash of the news cycle and the short attention spans exacerbated [made worse] by the Twitterification of politics worked against those efforts."[62] She went on to explain how the hashtag #DAPL was quickly replaced by conversations about the Academy Awards nominations.

Millions of people checked into the Oceti Sakowin Camp, shown here, in an attempt to support protesters fighting the Dakota Access Pipeline.

Are Online Petitions Effective?

There are many online petition websites that are not associated with the government. Change.org, for example, has more than 100 million users in 196 countries. Many signers of petitions receive criticism from others because it is one of the most widely used slacktivism activities.

Change.org's website claims to achieve one victory per hour with their petitions; some examples include a petition to the grocery chain Whole Foods signed by 110,000 people to push the corporation to fight food waste in the United States and a petition to the website building platform Squarespace signed by 60,000 to remove websites that host white supremacist content.

Some people are skeptical of Change.org's claim. Using the content analyzing tool BuzzSumo, reporter Amelia Tait looked at the top 10 petitions in Britain during 2016. She figured that the top 10, which had the most signatures, would be most likely to be successful. However, none of those petitions created any kind of change.

Top 10 British Online Petitions Throughout 2016 and Their Outcomes

Petition	Signatures	Shares	Outcome
EU Referendum Rules triggering a 2nd EU Referendum	4,150,260	785.7k	debated September 5, **unsuccessful**
Give the Meningitis B vaccine to ALL children, not just newborn babies	823,348	536.3k	debated April 25, **unsuccessful**
Block Donald J Trump from UK entry	586,930	379.7k	debated January 18, **unsuccessful**
Ban the sale of fireworks to the public and only approve organised displays	149,992	288.3k	not debated, **unsuccessful**
Close all retail on boxing day, retail isn't needed on boxing day!	144,453	278k	debated December 12, **unsuccessful**
Consider a vote of No Confidence in Jeremy Hunt, Health Secretary	339,925	252.6k	not debated, **unsuccessful**
No more school penalty fines and bring back the 10 day authorised absence	204,790	180.3k	debated July 11, **unsuccessful**
Free childcare when both parents are working. Not just those who are on benefits	133,921	176k	debated November 21, **unsuccessful**
Reverse the ESA disability benefit cut	136,890	145.6k	not debated, **unsuccessful**
Hold a General Election in 2016	177,014	135.6k	not debated, **unsuccessful**

Online petitions may get a lot of signatures, but they do not always get results, as this information from NewStatesman magazine shows.

Dismissing online petitions altogether might be dangerous, though—after all, they represent a large majority of public opinion and voting priorities. Many people believe petition websites and online activism have the power to make a huge impact when looked at as a whole rather than each individual signature or post. Joel Penney, a professor of communication and media at Montclair State University, wrote, "Although each individual act of posting, linking, commenting and liking may look insignificant up close, at a macro level [all together] they add up to nothing less than the networked spread of ideas."[63]

The information age has given humans the ability to have a real-time influence on policies and social interactions. Small comments from different people have shaped a collective narrative that directly corresponds to the way individuals behave in the world. Online activism encourages active citizenship because issues become regularly apparent in the constantly changing channels of communication.

Active citizenship, Jonathan Tisch wrote, is about

> taking part in the life of the community, not out of noblesse oblige [the feeling that having privilege comes with a sense of responsibility to help others] but because you care about the health of the society in which you live and share a responsibility for its future with every other citizen. Active citizenship doesn't just mean giving time to the local soup kitchen on a Saturday night (although efforts like that may be helpful, even admirable); it also means examining the root causes of problems like hunger and considering the entire range of actions you can take as a citizen to help eliminate those causes. Where volunteerism tries to alleviate the symptoms, active citizenship strives to cure the disease.[64]

Active citizenship can work on the internet, too. Online activism has the power to be extremely effective in social activism, yet in order for it to be successful, it must go beyond the digital world.

CHAPTER 5

How to Be an Online Activist

There is no doubt that social media will continue to shape social and political activism in the coming years. It is important for activists to understand how to use the tools they have to reach a broader audience, especially since many people are turning to online data to get information. However, being a successful online activist is generally not as simple as logging in and posting. To be the most helpful and responsible activist possible, certain considerations must be taken into account.

Organic Reach and Responsibility

Some marketing strategists believe that with the large amount of social media posts, in the future it will become difficult for social media campaigns to actually reach individuals with their posts. With Facebook actively trying to tailor a person's newsfeed to their interests, many organizations do not have a large organic reach, which is visibility that comes just by sharing as opposed to using paid advertisements. For instance, a page with 10,000 fans might expect only 650 of them to actually see a post.

Business experts who study social media behavior offer ways to counteract this problem. Activists can also use these strategies, such as being selective and informed to post only the best material, by publishing posts at peak user hours, and by focusing on long-term goals.

In 2015, four years after the Arab Spring, Wael Ghonim took the stage at a TED Talk to explain that while social media facilitated the Egyptian Revolution, it had also created a toxic environment after the government was overthrown. Polarization, or a large gap in opinions, between two party lines created a toxic environment. Trolls and hate speech were all over the internet and continue to be found today. According to Ghonim, "While it's true that polarization is primarily driven by our human behavior, social media shapes this behavior and magnifies its impact ... We need to figure out how technology can be part of the solution rather than part of the problem."[65]

Ghonim made the point that on the internet, it is easy to forget that there are real people engaging in dialogue. Most conversations, photos, and videos are curated on the internet, meaning people present themselves and their ideas in a very specific way. People also often see the comments and posts of others who have the same views, and when a different view is presented, things can become hateful quickly. People can block others or unfriend them with just one click. As Ghonim explained, people on the internet often talk *at* one another rather than *with* one another.

These negative communications will continue to exist on the internet for the foreseeable future as people repost, link, and search for keywords in search bars. It can be easy to become discouraged while trying to make a positive impact in the world and online, especially in light of these communication challenges. However, there are ways to combat the negatives and stay mentally and emotionally healthy.

#IRL

#IRL (in real life) started, as many internet hashtags do, as a meme. People were posting laughable comments and photos to reflect their circumstances or mental states, sometimes serious and sometimes ironic. What is interesting about the phrase is that it points out the separate worlds of online and offline. Many people talk about the two presences as though they are different from one another, but in reality, the online personality is just an extension of the person in the physical world. When someone is talking to another person online, it is important to remember that they are both still human beings with different perspectives and flaws—unless, of course, one happens to be a bot.

Being a Good Digital Citizen

Digital citizenship is a growing movement around the world. Also called digital wellness or digital ethics, digital citizenship is the practice of using the internet and technology in a responsible way. This means not only protecting private information and creative property, it also means engaging with others online in a smart and respectful way.

Even though activists are engaging in online and offline activities that call into question the actions of governments, corporations, or society in general, it is still important to maintain good digital citizenship. Activists should focus on facts—even when a topic is an emotional one—and they should also engage in respectful dialogue.

One example of a young activist who uses good digital citizenship practices is Hannah Alper, who started a blog in 2012 when she was nine years old. Alper built a huge following for her blog, and she has also become a motivational speaker. She started to promote Kindraising, a movement to change the world through kindness. Alper wrote, "I want to be part of creating a culture of kindness that will replace hate, indifference and apathy [lack of interest]. If we do this, we can be on the path to eliminating bullying and other issues that can be helped with positive actions."[66]

By posting and commenting on the positive impact of kindness on the world, Alper is doing her part to make the internet and the world a nicer place. Even while promoting issues she cares about, such as anti-bullying, she maintains a positive attitude that helps bring people to her cause.

Hannah Alper, shown above, is a young internet activist. She started a blog when she was nine years old, and her mission has been to stop bullying and to spread messages of kindness.

Going Viral

Just because it is easy to get online does not mean it is easy to be an activist online. With so many voices competing for attention, it takes more than digital savviness to win the hearts and minds of followers. It takes a long-term game plan, and it takes luck. Internet activism can be very powerful, but it is only one means of communication in a toolkit of activist techniques. Still, things do get incredibly popular on the internet, which can be both good and bad, depending on the situation.

When something is shared at such a fast pace that all of a sudden many people seem to know about it, it is said to have "gone viral." The 2014 ALS Ice Bucket Challenge is one such campaign. In the summer of 2014, more than 17 million people participated in a viral post that challenged users to dump a bucket of ice water over their heads or donate money for research into amyotrophic lateral sclerosis (ALS), also known as Lou Gehrig's disease. ALS is a rare neurological disease that affects the brain and spinal cord and causes patients to lose the ability to control their bodies, all while the mind remains active. Most people with the disease can expect to live only two to five years after diagnosis.

When professional golfer Chris Kennedy challenged his sister Jeanette Senerchia to do the Ice Bucket Challenge, two men saw it on her Facebook page: Pat Quinn in Yonkers, New York, and Pete Frates in Boston, Massachusetts, both of whom were diagnosed with the fatal disease and who are credited with promoting the ALS Ice Bucket Challenge.

Frates, a former baseball player, asked his doctor when he was diagnosed with ALS how much money it would take to find a cure. The answer was $1 billion. Frates set that amount as his goal. Quinn admitted he did not know anything about the disease when he was diagnosed. He said, "If I didn't know, I figured others didn't know either."[67] Both of these young men started to share the ALS Ice Bucket Challenge with friends and family and on social media. Celebrities such as Oprah Winfrey, Sir Patrick Stewart, Kristen Stewart, Channing Tatum, and many more got involved.

Before the ALS Ice Bucket Challenge, ALS was a disease that had not gotten much attention. Seventy-five years before the challenge, the famous baseball player Lou Gehrig was diagnosed. Since his diagnosis, there had not been much progress made in curing the disease. Experts still do not know what causes it or how to cure it.

Nearly $220 million was raised for various ALS research organizations during this viral campaign. The social media posts brought great awareness to the disease—and they also brought people with vital skills together. "That is for sure what the Ice Bucket campaign did … it brought in all these great biologists, engineers, people who never thought about ALS, into the ALS field,"[68] said Dr. Merit Cudkowicz, Frates's doctor.

Shown here are students of Endicott College in Massachusetts in their attempt to break the record for the number of participants in a single Ice Bucket Challenge.

During the next few years, there were various breakthroughs in research, including the discovery of an ALS gene and the release of new drugs, one of which would slow the progression of the disease up to 33 percent. This has the possibility of extending the life of a patient for a year or more.

Know What Is Being Posted

While going viral is certainly a boost for an activist campaign, it should not be the only goal. There is no blueprint for creating viral content, so activists cannot focus all their energies on making viral postings. Making real, personal connections and changing the actions and minds of a small number of individuals is a worthwhile task in its own right.

When reporting on a situation or making a post for a campaign on social media, it is important for activists to make sure they are never posting without thinking critically about the post itself. As the post will be a representation of the person or campaign long after it is made, it is good practice to consider the long-term effects of a statement. Campaigns that are built on emotional statements and ideas can manipulate a person into saying something without thinking, which sometimes hurts the ideals they are trying to protect. In these cases, going viral is not a good thing.

For example, in 2012, the 30-minute film *Kony 2012*, produced by Invisible Children, Inc., went viral. The hashtag #KONY2012 began to show up in newsfeeds, and within six days of the March 5, 2012, release of the film, *Kony 2012* had received more than 100 million views. The film presented a clear enemy in Joseph Kony, the leader of the Lord's Resistance Army (LRA) out of Uganda, which was made up of child soldiers. Kony had been indicted by the International Criminal Court for war crimes and human rights violations. The goal of *Kony 2012* was to raise awareness of this problem, make Kony hated, and get him arrested by the end of 2012. Invisible Children succeeded in raising awareness as well as money but failed in its aim of getting Kony arrested, although the organization was clear that this goal was secondary to raising awareness of the problems of child soldiers and conflict in Uganda. According to *Slate*, "The group existed to raise funds to make films, which raised more funds, which it spent raising more awareness. But young supporters were surprised to learn that just a third of Invisible Children's funds went to programs that directly served Ugandans."[69] These are the same criticisms aimed at slacktivism: raising awareness of a problem without taking any steps to improve the problem.

Kony 2012, despite its popularity, received many bad reviews. Critics argued that the film was "inaccurate, oversimplified, and distracting from more effective charity work in Uganda."[70] Some very large criticisms were thrown at the film: that it exaggerated the scale of abductions and the use of child soldiers, that the LRA and Kony are no longer in Uganda and that their numbers have shrunk significantly, that Invisible Children wasted its donors' money, and that the campaign ignored inconvenient facts and created a scenario in which the Western world had to go in and save the native people. This last accusation so enraged some Ugandans that rocks were thrown at the screen during a public viewing.

Some Questions to Ask Before Posting Online

1. Am I posting about something when I should be taking action?
2. Have I done fact-checking with at least three sources?
3. Will I be okay with everyone I know (and those I don't) reading this a year or a few years from now?
4. Am I willing to face any real-life consequences that may occur if my post goes viral?

The stress of marketing the video became very challenging, so much so that one of the filmmakers, Jason Russell, was arrested after having a mental breakdown in which he appeared naked in public. He told *Today,* "It was so chaotic. It was so exciting because it felt like the world was for us, and then at the same time it was heartbreaking and felt almost like a nightmare because it felt like the world was against us."[71] The campaign became a joke among Westerners, but as *Slate* pointed out, it "left a lasting mark on young people's political consciousness. That the mark has nothing to do with human rights atrocities in Uganda is a lesson in the limits of awareness pursued at the expense of truth."[72]

Invisible Children's nonprofit campaign Kony 2012 went viral much more quickly than the activists had anticipated.

All this is a lesson for activists in planning and forethought, both in regard to the people they are trying to convince and the people they are trying to help. For supporters, it is a lesson in knowing what they are supporting before sharing or donating. Fact-checking is an important element of traditional reporting that should not be lost. Before believing something on social media, make sure multiple sources are saying the same thing, and make sure those sources are credible. Any activist campaign is hurt when, in an attempt to make the alternate view look bad or to gain more supporters, incorrect facts are stated.

Getting Off the Internet

There is no doubt that social media will continue to shape the future of activism both on and off the screen. While physical forms of protests—such as rallies, sit-ins, marches, and arrests—will likely not stop any time soon, many forms of civil disobedience will shift to the internet, where anyone has the power to impact social change.

Zeynep Tufekci, the computer programmer from Turkey, believes social media is a great way to get attention and change the narrative but that it is not a good way for like-minded people to organize. She told the Sierra Club, "What's missing is collective decision-making in a manner that fits the participatory sensibilities of today's activists."[73] She went on to say that while activists jump at new technologies that would help reach more people, they are stuck where the most people hang out—on websites such as Facebook and Twitter.

Online activism is only as good as the people behind the computer screen, and that means that in order for it to jump-start meaningful conversations and actions, it has to go beyond the computer; it has to escape the digital borders and enter the physical world.

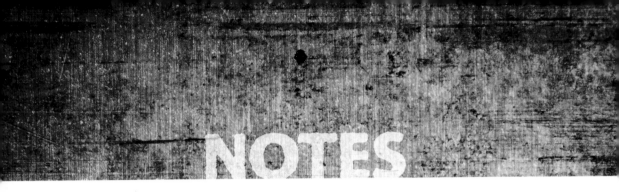

Introduction: The Arab Spring

1. Nadia Idle and Alex Nunns, eds., *Tweets from Tahrir: Egypt's Revolution as It Unfolded, in the Words of the People Who Made It.* New York, NY: OR Books, 2011, p. 13.

2. Idle and Nunns, *Tweets from Tahrir*, p. 12.

3. Wael Ghonim, "Inside the Egyptian Revolution," TEDTalk video, 10:01, March 2011. www.ted.com/talks/wael_ghonim_inside_the_egyptian_revolution.

4. Quoted in Catherine O'Donnell, "New Study Quantified Use of Social Media in Arab Spring," University of Washington, September 12, 2011. www.washington.edu/news/2011/09/12/new-study-quantifies-use-of-social-media-in-arab-spring/.

5. Parvez Sharma, "Egypt Is Burning, and It Is Not a Facebook or Twitter Event," *Huffington Post*, accessed on November 27, 2017. www.huffingtonpost.com/parvez-sharma/egypt-is-burning-and-it-i_b_815605.html.

6. Malcolm Gladwell, "Does Egypt Need Twitter?," *New Yorker*, February 2, 2011. www.newyorker.com/news/news-desk/does-egypt-need-twitter.

7. Quoted in Nicholas Thompson, "Is Twitter Helping in Egypt?," *New Yorker*, January 27, 2011. www.newyorker.com/news/news-desk/is-twitter-helping-in-egypt.

8. Tim Eaton, "Internet Activism and the Egyptian Uprisings: Transforming Online Dissent Into the Offline World," *Westminster Press*, vol. 9, no. 2, 2013, p. 5.

9. Idle and Nunns, *Tweets from Tahrir*, p. 19.

Chapter 1: The History of Online Activism

10. Justin Hall, "Web Story," links.net, accessed on November 27, 2017. links.net/vita/web/story.html.

11. "About We the People," We the People, accessed on November 28, 2017. petitions.whitehouse.gov/about.

12. Paul Hilton, "'We the People': Five Years of Online Petitions," Pew Research Center, December 28, 2016. www.pewinternet. org/2016/12/28/white-house-responses-and-policy-impact-of-petitions.

13. Quoted in Rachel Weiner, "White House Rejects 'Death Star' Petition," *Washington Post*, January 12, 2013. www. washingtonpost.com/news/post-politics/wp/2013/01/12/white-house-rejects-death-star-petittion/?utm_term=.8fb5052ecc3b.

14. Adi Robertson, "Will Donald Trump Keep the White House Petition Site Alive?," Verge, March 22, 2017. www.theverge. com/2017/3/22/15022050/donald-trump-white-house-petition-we-the-people-update.

Chapter 2: How Online Activism Works

15. Quoted in Cindy Sui, "Will the Sunflower Movement Change Taiwan?," BBC, April 9, 2015. www.bbc.com/news/world-asia-32157210.

16. Tyler Mahoney, "Citizen Journalism Needs a Dose of Journalistic Ethics After Sandy," *Huffington Post*, November 6, 2012. www.huffingtonpost.com/tyler-mahoney/hurricane-sandy-citizen-journalism_b_2082596.html.

17. Caitlin Dewey, "The Next Frontier of Online Activism Is 'Woke' Chatbots," *Washington Post*, August 11, 2016. www.washingtonpost.com/news/the-intersect/wp/2016/08/11/ the-next-frontier-of-online-activism-is-woke-chatbots/?utm_ term=.71ec711154f8.

18. Larry Atkins, "States Should Require Schools to Teach Media Literacy To Combat Fake News," *Huffington Post*, July 13, 2017. www.huffingtonpost.com/entry/states-should-require-schools-to-teach-media-literacy_us_59676573e4b07b5e1d96ed86.

19. Steve Lambert, "Make Capitalism Work for Me!," Kickstarter, accessed on November 28, 2017. www.kickstarter.com/projects/ slambert/make-capitalism-work-for-me/description.

20. Jonathan M. Tisch, *Citizen You: How Social Entrepreneurs Are Changing the World.* New York, NY: Three Rivers Press, 2010, p. 130.

21. Tisch, *Citizen You*, p. 131.

22. Donald Trump (@realDonaldTrump), Twitter, July 1, 2017, 3:41 p.m. twitter.com/realDonaldTrump/status/881281755017355264.

23. Donald Trump (@realDonaldTrump), Twitter, November 2017, 4:48 p.m. twitter.com/realdonaldtrump/status/929511061954297857?lang=en.

24. Quoted in John Haltiwanger, "Twitter Founder Says Donald Trump Proves Social Media Makes People Dumber," *Newsweek*, September 13, 2017. www.newsweek.com/twitter-founder-says-trump-proves-social-media-makes-people-dumber-664277.

25. Heather Smith, "Has the Internet Changed Activism?," Sierra Club, May 10, 2017. www.sierraclub.org/sierra/has-internet-changed-activism.

26. Scott Shane, "The Fake Americans Russia Created to Influence the Election," *New York Times*, September 7, 2017. www.nytimes.com/2017/09/07/us/politics/russia-facebook-twitter-election.html.

27. Quoted in Max Read, "Does Even Mark Zuckerberg Know What Facebook Is?," *New York Magazine*, October 1, 2017. nymag.com/selectall/2017/10/does-even-mark-zuckerberg-know-what-facebook-is.html.

28. Mark Zuckerberg, "Bringing the World Closer Together," Facebook, June 22, 2017. www.facebook.com/notes/mark-zuckerberg/bringing-the-world-closer-together/10154944663901634/.

29. Quoted in Eric Johnson, "To Fix Politics, You Have to Fix Fundraising, Crowdpac CEO Steve Hilton Says," Recode, April 19, 2017. www.recode.net/2017/4/19/15350312/steve-hilton-crowdpac-politics-fundraising-recode-podcast.

Chapter 3: Grassroots Activism

30. Quoted in Heather Gautney, "What Is Occupy Wall Street? The History of Leaderless Movements," *Washington Post*, October 10, 2011. www.washingtonpost.com/national/on-leadership/what-is-occupy-wall-street-the-history-of-leaderless-movements/2011/10/10/gIQAwkFjaL_story.html?utm_term=.0852dde8ca03.

31. Quoted in "To Occupy Wall Street, Occupy the Internet First," Reuters, October 4, 2011. www.reuters.com/article/wallstreet-protests-media/to-occupy-wall-street-occupy-the-internet-first-idUSN1E7930OC20111004.

32. Ben Berkowitz, "From a Single Hashtag, a Protest Circled the World," Reuters, October 17, 2011. www.reuters.com/article/us-wallstreet-protests-social/from-a-single-hashtag-a-protest-circled-the-world-idUSTRE79G6E420111018.

33. Quoted in Megan Leonhardt, "The Lasting Effects of Occupy Wall Street, Five Years Later," *TIME*, September 16, 2016. time.com/money/4495707/occupy-wall-street-anniversary-effects/.

34. Tarana Burke, "The Inception," Just Be, Inc., accessed on November 29, 2017. justbeinc.wixsite.com/justbeinc/the-me-too-movement-cmml.

35. Alyssa Milano (@Alyssa_Milano), Twitter, October 15, 2017, 1:21 PM. twitter.com/alyssa_milano/status/919659438700670976.

36. Sophie Gilbert, "The Movement of #MeToo," *The Atlantic*, October 16, 2017. www.theatlantic.com/entertainment/archive/2017/10/the-movement-of-metoo/542979/.

37. Wesley Lowery, *"They Can't Kill Us All": The Story of the Struggle for Black Lives*. New York, NY: Hachette Book Group, 2016, p. 82.

38. Lowery, *"They Can't Kill Us All,"* p. 84.

39. Quoted in Lowery, *"They Can't Kill Us All,"* p. 86.

40. Quoted in Lowery, *"They Can't Kill Us All,"* p. 39.

41. Quoted in Lowery, *"They Can't Kill Us All,"* p. 39.

Chapter 4: Hacktivism and Slacktivism

42. "10 Anonymous Triumphs," Anonymous video, 11:12, July 2, 2016. anonofficial.com/anonymous-10-anonymous-triumphs.

43. Quoted in Waqas, "Anonymous Nailed 2015," Hackread, January 1, 2016. www.hackread.com/anonymous-nailed-2015/.

44. Quoted in Laura Petrecca, "Steubenville Rape Case Driven by Social Media," *USA Today*, March 18, 2013. www.usatoday.com/story/news/2013/03/18/steubenville-rape-social-media-football/1997687/.

45. Quoted in David Kushner, "Anonymous vs. Steubenville," *Rolling Stone*, November 27, 2013. www.rollingstone.com/culture/news/anonymous-vs-steubenville-20131127.

46. Quoted in Kushner, "Anonymous vs. Steubenville."

47. Raffi Khatchadourian, "Julian Assange, A Man Without a Country," *New Yorker*, August 21, 2017. www.newyorker.com/magazine/2017/08/21/julian-assange-a-man-without-a-country.

48. Quoted in Maya Rhodan, "White House Responds to Petition Urging Obama to Pardon Edward Snowden," *TIME*, July 28, 2015. time.com/3974713/white-house-edward-snowden-petition/.

49. Quoted in Rhodan, "White House Responds to Petition."

50. Amanda Dixon, "What Is a Shell Company?," SmartAsset, May 27, 2016. smartasset.com/investing/what-is-a-shell-company.

51. Jake Bernstein, "Journalist Explains How Panama Papers Opened Up the World's Illicit Money Networks," *Fresh Air*, NPR, November 20, 2017. www.npr.org/2017/11/20/565319852/journalist-explains-how-panama-papers-opened-up-the-worlds-illicit-money-network.

52. Kate Knibbs, "Slacktivists, Unite! Social Media Campaigns Aren't Just Feel-Good Back Patting," Digital Trends, May 15, 2013. www.digitaltrends.com/opinion/slacktivists-unite-social-media-campaigns-arent-just-feel-good-back-patting/.

53. Quoted in Rosalie Tostevin, "Online Activism: It's Easy to Click, but Just as Easy to Disengage," *Guardian*, March 14, 2014. www.theguardian.com/media-network/media-network-blog/2014/mar/14/online-activism-social-media-engage.

54. Andrea Vale, "Voices: Why I'm Not Changing My Profile Picture to the French Flag," *USA Today College*, November 16, 2015. college.usatoday.com/2015/11/16/voices-why-im-not-changing-my-profile-picture-to-the-french-flag/.

55. Quoted in David Mikkelson, "Bra Color as Facebook Status," Snopes, December 6, 2010. www.snopes.com/computer/internet/bracolor.asp.

56. Quoted in Susan Donaldson James, "Bra Color Status on Facebook Goes Viral," ABC News, January 8, 2010. abcnews.go.com/Health/bra-color-status-facebook-raises-curiosity-money-viral/story?id=9513986.

57. Quoted in James, "Bra Color Status on Facebook Goes Viral."

58. Hortense Smith, "Thanks for Sharing, but Your Bra Color Isn't Going To Cure Cancer," *Jezebel*, January 9, 2010. jezebel. com/5444444/thanks-for-sharing-but-your-bra-color-isnt-going-to-cure-cancer.

59. Quoted in Madison Malone Kircher, "Checking in at Standing Rock on Facebook Is a Nice Show of Solidarity, and Not Much Else," *New York Magazine*, October 31, 2016. nymag. com/selectall/2016/10/north-dakota-standing-rock-pipeline-facebook-check-in-hoax.html.

60. Kircher, "Checking in at Standing Rock on Facebook."

61. Quoted in Alexis Kleinman, "Checking in at Standing Rock on Facebook Isn't Helpful—Here's What You Can Do Instead," *Mic*, October 31, 2016. mic.com/articles/158162/standing-rock-facebook-check-in-dakota-access-pipeline-protest-isnt-helpful-what-you-can-do#.NSEch3ZcF.

62. Emily Dreyfuss, "Social Media Made the World Care About Standing Rock—and Helped It Forget," *Wired*, January 24, 2017. www.wired.com/2017/01/social-media-made-world-care-standing-rock-helped-forget/.

63. Joel Penney, "More than 'Slacktivism': We Dismiss the Power of Politics Online at Our Peril," The Conversation, August 1, 2017. theconversation.com/more-than-slacktivism-we-dismiss-the-power-of-politics-online-at-our-peril-79500.

64. Tisch, *Citizen You*, p. 10.

Chapter 5: How to Be an Online Activist

65. Ghonim, "Let's Design Social Media That Drives Real Change."

66. Hannah Alper, "About Kindraising," Kindraising, accessed on November 30, 2017. kindraising.callmehannah.ca/about-kindraising/.

67. Quoted in "8 Questions with Pat Quinn, an ALS Patient and Advocate," Innovation, September 12, 2017. innovation. org/2017/09/12/8-questions-pat-quinn-als-patient-advocate/.

68. Quoted in Juju Chang, John Kapetaneas, and Jasmine Brown, "How a Former Baseball Player's Fight Against ALS Led to the Ice Bucket Challenge Internet Sensation," ABC News, September 28, 2017. abcnews.go.com/Health/baseball-players-fight-als-ice-bucket-challenge-internet/story?id=50152750.

69. Christina Cauterucci, "The Lessons of Kony 2012," Slate, September 16, 2016. www.slate.com/articles/news_and_politics/the_next_20/2016/09/kony_2012_quickly_became_a_punch_line_but_what_if_it_did_more_good_than.html.

70. Nick Thompson, "'KONY 2012' Viral Video Raises Questions about Filmmakers," CNN, March 12, 2012. www.cnn.com/2012/03/09/world/africa/kony-2012-q-and-a/index.html.

71. Quoted in Matt Williams, "Kony 2012 Campaigner Jason Russell: 'I Wasn't in Control of My Mind or Body,'" Guardian, October 8, 2012. www.theguardian.com/world/2012/oct/08/kony-2012-jason-russell-interview-nbc.

72. Cauterucci, "The Lessons of Kony 2012."

73. Quoted in Smith, "Has the Internet Changed Activism?"

DISCUSSION QUESTIONS

Chapter 1: The History of Online Activism

1. How has the internet changed communication?

2. How has communication between people remained the same?

3. What, in your opinion, are the most effective communication channels?

Chapter 2: How Online Activism Works

1. Do you think a president should use a personal social media account? Why or why not?

2. What makes online activism so powerful?

3. In what ways has social media changed politics? What are some positive and negative outcomes?

Chapter 3: Grassroots Activism

1. Do you think Occupy Wall Street was successful? Why or why not?

2. What is your opinion of the effectiveness of social media activism campaigns?

3. Why do you think opinions of Black Lives Matter are so polarized?

Chapter 4: Hacktivism and Slacktivism

1. Do you think hashtags and online petitions are useful?

2. Do you think WikiLeaks helps or harms the public? Why?

3. Do you think leaderless movements such as Anonymous are successful?

Chapter 5: How to Be an Online Activist

1. Why do you think the ALS Ice Bucket Challenge was so successful?

2. Have you ever created an activist post?

3. How can you be a good digital citizen while also being an activist?

ORGANIZATIONS TO CONTACT

Demand Progress
30 Ritchie Avenue
Silver Spring, MD 20910
contact@demandprogress.org
www.demandprogress.org
> This is a grassroots nonprofit organization that has
> 2 million affiliated activists focusing on civil liberties, civil
> rights, and government reform. The organization is also an
> example of a campaign that uses online resources to further
> individual causes.

Fight for the Future
PO Box 55071 #95005
Boston, MA 02205
team@fightforthefuture.org
www.fightforthefuture.org
> This organization works to advance the effectiveness of
> online campaigns focusing on basic human rights and
> freedoms. It is a wonderful resource for ideas on specific
> online campaigns.

The Info-Activism How-To Guide
Tactical Technology Collective
Kingsfordweg 151
Amsterdam
1043 GR, Netherlands
ttc@tacticaltech.org
howto.informationactivism.org
> A great resource for putting together an activist campaign,
> this how-to guide offers basic instructions on creating con-
> tent, creating strategies, and using digital tools.

Reset: Digital and Online Activism

info@reset.org

en.reset.org/knowledge/digital-and-online-activism

>This organization, which is committed to digital sustainability, is a great way to learn about responsible online solutions. In addition, the organization offers up-to-date statistics and case studies on digital trends.

Voices of Youth

info@voicesofyouth.org

www.voicesofyouth.org/

>An organization set up by UNICEF, Voices of Youth is an online space for young people to discuss opinions and stories from around the globe. Its active forum is a great place to learn about what others think about a number of different topics. Always ask a parent or guardian before participating in an online forum.

FOR MORE INFORMATION

Books

Gay, Kathlyn. *Activism: The Ultimate Teen Guide*. Lanham, MD: Rowman & Littlefield, 2016.

> In the 21st century, many activist campaigns are driven by young people. This book provides a guide to help young adults get involved in causes they care about.

Idle, Nadia, and Alex Nunns, eds. *Tweets from Tahrir: Egypt's Revolution as it Unfolded, in the Words of the People Who Made It*. New York, NY: OR Books, 2011.

> This fascinating book shows the Egyptian revolution as it unfurled through the real-time tweets of citizens experiencing the movement.

Jenkins, Henry, et al. *By Any Media Necessary: The New Youth Activism*. New York, NY: New York University Press, 2016.

> This book examines the intersection of political and social life of America's youth through specific case studies. These young people are using new forms of technology to participate in the world and to engage in issues about which they are passionate.

Lowery, Wesley. *"They Can't Kill Us All": The Story of the Struggle for Black Lives*. New York, NY: Hachette Book Group, 2016.

> This book covers the feelings behind the Black Lives Matter movement, and it also offers valuable perspectives on race relations in the modern United States.

Tisch, Jonathan M. *Citizen You: How Social Entrepreneurs Are Changing the World*. New York, NY: Three Rivers Press, 2010.

> Emphasizing the role of citizens in social change, this book covers a number of valuable elements in the activist process, including how individuals can use social media to their advantage.

Websites

Activist Facts

www.activistfacts.com

Created by the Center for Organizational Research and Education, this website catalogues a list of nonprofits to give activists and donors the most up-to-date information.

Black Lives Matter

blacklivesmatter.com

This website is a good source for learning about the history of the Black Lives Matter movement as well as the group's mission and upcoming events.

Call Me Hannah

callmehannah.ca

Hannah Alper's personal website and blog discusses important world events as well as ways young people can get involved in activism.

Snopes

www.snopes.com

This is a good resource for fact-checking posts and news articles to improve digital literacy.

The Webby Awards

www.webbyawards.com

The Webby Awards were established in 1996. This website is a good place to keep up to date on innovators across the web and find information about leading internet activists.

INDEX

PICTURE CREDITS

Cover Ramin Talaie/Corbis via Getty Images; p.7 Mohamed Elsayyed/Shutterstock.com; p. 8 Niall Carson/PA Images via Getty Images; p. 10 Chris Hondros/Getty Images; p. 12 Jürgen Ritter/ullstein bild via Getty Images; p. 14 © istockphoto.com/GeorgiosArt; p. 15 Everett Historical/ Shutterstock.com; p. 17 courtesy of the Library of Congress; p. 18 Stock image/Shutterstock.com; p. 19 Jeff Morris—PA Images/PA Images via Getty Images; p. 23 sitthiphong/ Shutterstock.com; p. 26 Stefan Rousseau—PA Images/PA Images via Getty Images; p. 30 Craig Ferguson/LightRocket via Getty Images; p. 32 View Apart/Shutterstock.com; p. 35 ANDER GILLENEA/AFP/Getty Images; p. 46 lev radin/ Shutterstock.com; p. 51 Ira Bostic/Shutterstock.com; p. 55 a katz/Shutterstock.com; p. 57 Africa Studio/Shutterstock.com; p. 61 Chris Harvey/Shutterstock.com; p. 63 Spencer Platt/Getty Images; p. 65 MATTHEW MIRABELLI/AFP/Getty Images; p. 66 Chip Somodevilla/Getty Images; p. 68 BEN STANSALL/ AFP/Getty Images; p. 74 Photo Image/Shutterstock.com; p. 79 Dominik Magdziak Photography/Getty Images; p. 81 John Blanding/The Boston Globe via Getty Images; p. 84 Sandy Huffaker/Corbis via Getty Images.

ABOUT THE AUTHOR

Amanda Vink is an author and actress in Buffalo, NY. She received her bachelor's degree from the State University of New York at Fredonia in English and creative writing. She has written a number of books and has been involved in films that have won international awards. When not writing or acting, Amanda enjoys hiking, practicing the Dutch language, and learning to play the bagpipes.